Domestic Violence in America

Domestic Violence in America

V. Michael McKenzie, Ph.D., C.A.C.

Brunswick

Copyright © 1995 by V. Michael McKenzie, Ph.D., C.A.C.

Library of Congress Cataloging-in-Publication Data

McKenzie, V. Michael, 1947–
 Domestic violence in America / V. Michael McKenzie.
  p. cm.
 Includes bibliographical references (p.) and index.
 ISBN 1–55618–151–5 (hard cover : alk. paper)
 1. Family violence—United States—Prevention. 2. Wife abuse—United States—Prevention. 3. Abused women—Services for—United States. 4. Abusive men—Counseling of—United States. 5. Abusive men—Rehabilitation—United States. I. Title.
HQ809.3.U5M39 1995
362.82'92'0973—dc20   95–14147
                 CIP

First Edition
Published in the United States of America
by

Brunswick Publishing Corporation
1386 Lawrenceville Plank Road
Lawrenceville, Virginia 23868

Dedication

This book is dedicated to the victims and survivors of spousal battery, and other types of domestic violence. Reach deep within, and find the courage to extricate yourself from the purgatory of abuse. The transition from victim to survivor is the greatest gift you can bestow upon yourself. Change now! Today.

This dedication also extends to victim advocates, and spousal battery counselors—your dedicated efforts are making a recognizable difference in the lives of victimized persons.

Acknowledgment

This book began as a scholarly and solitary effort. Its fruition emanated from encouragement and support of family, friends, and colleagues. I would like to thank Ms. Lynette Belle for her invaluable contribution. Mrs. Francine McKenzie labored tirelessly on proofreading and references. Ms. Serujnie Subick was not only creative with her word processor, she graciously tolerated the revisions thrusted upon her. I thank you both for your patience, tolerance, and creative input.

To my mentors: Penny Morrill, RN, Executive Director, Sunrise Domestic Violence Center, and the Honorable Judge Lynn Tepper, 6th Judicial Circuit, Dade City, Florida, I thank you for the continued inspiration in your dedicated work with victims and survivors, and educating of professionals and our citizenry. Special thanks to Dr. Walter J. Raymond, Mrs. Marianne S. Raymond, and staff for the constructive editorial guidance. I thank my parents Mr. and Mrs. Charles and Ellen McKenzie for their encouragement and support. Poet Dee Brown of California, thanks for the practical information.

Robin S. Hassler, Esq., Executive Director, Governor's Task Force on Domestic Violence, and Kathy Daniels, Program Coordinator, deserve special thanks for their commendable work on the Governor's Task Force and Batterers' Commission including the voluminous spousal battery material to which I had access. The clinical team— Sally Berger, B.S., Janet DiResta-Fox, M.A., C.R.C., and Ronald Parker, M.A.,—merits special thanks for their collegial longevity. My appreciation and thanks to evaluative readers: Dr. Beverly Belle, Dr. William Hutchison, Jr., and Dr. Chester M. Pierce.

The McKenzie Family—thanks to Michelle, Rhonda, Mikey, Rochelle, Kris, and Phillip, with special mention of Ny-Asha—I appreciate your inspiration and constructive criticism.

Table of Contents

Foreword

Through his book, *Domestic Violence in America*, Dr. V. Michael McKenzie has produced a comprehensive guide on contemporary approaches for understanding the causes and state-of-the-art approaches to the treatment of domestic violence.

In the first four chapters, the extent of the problem is outlined along with descriptions of biological, psychological, and social factors that contribute to the "making of a batterer." Chapter Five through Eleven outlined various intervention approaches designed to break the spousal battery cycle, including the key role of law enforcement, the judicial, and medical systems. The principles of treatment advanced by the author focus on ending spousal battery by teaching the batterer anger management skills, and changing his need to control. The emphasis on health, survival, and empowered assertiveness underscores key elements in Dr. McKenzie's concept for the victims becoming "empowered survivors."

Helping professionals in medicine, law, nursing, teaching, social work, rehabilitation counseling; students of contemporary society, victims, and perpetrators of domestic violence will find this book most informative and helpful.

Extensive references and a comprehensive directory of domestic violence resources conclude this outstanding book.

William S. Hutchison, Jr., M.S.W., Ph.D.
Professor of Social Work, University of
South Florida, Department of Social Work
College of Social and Behavioral Services
Tampa, Florida 33620

Over the years, I have read many books about domestic violence, but this is the first I have seen that has value for *all* the disciplines that interface with the issue. It is clearly written, easily understood, and well documented. Further, *Domestic Violence in America* has some new interventions in dealing with victims and perpetrators. On the other hand, the book is broad enough in scope to be a valuable educational tool for one's own learning or to utilize in educating groups about the issue of domestic violence. I am truly very impressed by this comprehensive piece of work, and yet come away from reading without feeling overburdened.

Penny Morrill, RN, Executive Director,
Sunrise Domestic Violence Center
Dade City, Florida

Domestic Violence in America is a practical, informative comprehensive and easy to read synthesis of what is known about and how to approach one of the searing problems of our time.

I particularly like the author's plethora of data and the multidisciplinary emphasis. Further, I think it is written so that it will be helpful to experts from different walks of life, as well as interested lay persons. The conceptualizations, graphics, statistics, references and directories make this book especially valuable.

Chester M. Pierce, M.D., Sc.D.
Professor of Psychiatry and Education
Faculty of Medicine and Graduate School
of Education, Harvard University
Cambridge, Massachusetts

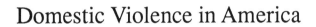
Domestic Violence in America

Introduction

In September 1993, Florida's Governor Lawton Chiles demonstrated his continued leadership on women and family issues by convening the state's first task force on domestic violence—named the Governor's Domestic Violence Implementation Task Force. In its January 1994 report, the Task Force recommended that a Commission on Minimum Standards for Batterers' Treatment be created to develop criteria that would govern batterers' treatment and intervention programs operating within the State of Florida.

The Florida Legislature created a Commission on Minimum Standards for Batterers' Treatment, and established it in the Office of the Governor. The Commission consisted of the following Governor's appointees: two persons with expertise in the treatment of batterers, one person from a state certified domestic violence center, one state attorney designee, one public defender designee, one certified addictions treatment professional, one person from a state or county probation program, one county judge, one circuit judge, one person from the military, one person from the state university system, and two others appointed at the discretion of the Governor.

In August 1994, I was appointed by Governor Lawton Chiles to this Commission in the capacity of a certified addictions treatment professional. The Commission met throughout the State of Florida, and took public testimony from victims and survivors, rehabilitated batterers, mental health practitioners, treatment program providers, judges, attorneys, domestic violence staff, and members of the public. The Commission solicited treatment protocols, and established

1

intervention criteria from batterers' programs throughout the nation. Many of these jurisdictions have already developed, implemented, monitored, and evaluated the effectiveness of their domestic violence intervention programs.

One of the major revelations that struck me again was the enormity of domestic violence in America, and its under-reported status. The first principal act undertaken by the Commission was to re-name itself from the Commission on Minimum Standards for Batterers' Treatment, to the Commission on Minimum Standards for Batterers' Intervention. The term "treatment" is in essence a misnomer regarding domestic violence. Those individuals who batter are rarely or seldom, if ever, sick or ill—hence requiring treatment. Spousal Battery is learned behavior perpetrated purposefully, deliberately, and intentionally to dominate, control, and exercise power over a spouse or partner. Chapter Four discusses how the family socialization process inculcates gender-biased beliefs, and behavior in youngsters that continue the intergenerational cycle of domestic violence.

The Commission rejected "treatment" because it implies intrinsic pathology or some psychological abnormality—thus inappropriately displacing causality and responsibility from the batterer to some other entity. The Commission found "intervention" to be the precise and preferred term because it involves interruption of the batterer's violent behavior, with an explicit opportunity for cognitive behavioral change.

There is another commonly held misbelief that couples' communication enhancement counseling, or anger man-agement intervention is effective in ameliorating spousal battery and abuse. No empirical evidence exists to substan-tiate this belief. Thus, the credible and efficacious batterers' programs focus specifically on the power and control inter-vention models.

Similarly, there is a popular misperception that alcohol, and prescription or illicit drug abuse cause spousal battery. Although a correlation exists between substance abuse and domestic violence, the ingestion of alcohol and drugs does not cause domestic violence. Research evidence has demonstrated that individuals, who use illicit drugs, and abuse alcohol and prescription medication are at a greater risk for perpetrating physical violence, emotional and psychological abuse on their spouse, children, and other family members.

Apart from placing the individual in a high risk category for spousal abuse, alcohol and drugs affect a person's cognitive functions such as memory, perception, reasoning and other thought processes. The individual's feelings and behavior are affected as well. So, when varying amounts of alcohol and/or drugs are in a person's system, he or she is likely to be unreasonable, irrational, short-tempered, impulsive, and easily angered. The individual may choose to batter a partner while under the influence of alcohol or drugs. If this person has a history of spousal battery, the alcohol and/or drugs can exacerbate benign conflict and increase the violent behavior. Unarguably, there are many individuals who drink alcohol and/or abuse drugs, but they do not batter their partner. Thus, this reinforces the point that substance abuse does not cause battery.

Spousal batterers who are episodic or chronic alcoholics and/or addicted to drugs, can be treated along with, but separate from the batterers' intervention program. Additionally, alcohol and drug counseling increases the likelihood that a reformed spousal batterer will discard his violence, and not engage in battery of his partner or children.

This book advances an interdisciplinary approach to the cessation of spousal battery. It synthesizes the role of mental health professionals, medical practitioners, law enforcement, the judiciary, and academia. Chapter One delineates the magnitude of domestic violence in our nation through statistical profiling of those most affected: women, children, the elderly, pregnant and culturally different individuals. Chapter Two presents the Spousal Battery Cycle, which represents the author's conceptualization of the phases of battery. Chapter Three addresses the beliefs of men who batter, risk factors, characteristics of victims including why they stay and how they fight back. Chapter Four looks at how the socialization process contributes to the personality of a batterer.

Intergender and intercultural communication is a vital part of the Intervention process. Chapter Five focuses on intergender and intercultural training. Chapters Six and Seven present the goals and outcome of skills training for law enforcement, the judiciary, and medical personnel. Rehabilitation of the batterer seeks to end spousal battery therapeutically through proven intervention techniques as reflected in Chapter Eight. Chapters Nine, Ten, and Eleven present the victim's transition to survivor, with the dynamics of healing and recovery. This book concludes with a nationwide directory of domestic violence centers including national hot lines for spousal battery victims and survivors.

V. Michael McKenzie, Ph.D., C.A.C.

Chapter One

Understanding Domestic Violence

Domestic violence is a progressively fatal, but preventable and treatable behavioral problem.

V. Michael McKenzie, Ph.D.

Heightened Awareness

Most of us were riveted to our seats, and glued to television sets in disbelief as a Ford Bronco raced down a California highway on June 17, 1994. The principal occupant was football giant O. J. Simpson. In the superstar's company was his faithful childhood friend Al Cowlings. In pursuit was an entourage of police cars and helicopters, and the undisciplined press corps seeking to capture America's celebrity double-murder suspect, and a sensational story respectively. As the news of O. J. Simpson's highway chase circulated on television, radio, and cellular telephones, Californians in the immediate vicinity took to the streets, and jubilantly cheered the fugitive and his companion. This spectacle marked the beginning of an international focus on the events surrounding the Simpson tragedy.

A focus on O. J. Simpson's apparent flight revealed an extensive history of domestic violence, wherein, O. J. reportedly battered his wife Nicole with impunity. The terror and exasperation in Nicole Brown-Simpson's voice, as she desperately beseeched 911 Emergency to intervene, frightened and enlightened a citizenry whose denial of the magnitude of domestic violence has facilitated its continuance. Whether they be police officers who refuse to arrest, prosecutors who fail to prosecute, judges who are reluctant to sentence, or other professionals and ordinary citizens unwilling to get involved, we have all failed to vociferously decry domestic violence in America. This failure to condemn domestic violence has poignantly communicated our complicity, tolerance, collusion, and acceptance of this barbarity. Domestic violence has laid dormant in our collective unconscious for decades. However, the Nicole Brown-Simpson's savage murder, and the shocking revelations of spousal battery by her ex-husband ignited mass outrage at the brutality of family violence.

Domestic Violence: The "Private Dirty Secret"

This national focus has transformed the obscure and underreported crime of domestic violence from the privately held "dirty secret" to a matter of international concern and public discourse. Many harbor the mistaken belief, and accompanying feeling that since domestic violence occurs in the private domain of intimate relationships, it is quite different from the random violence between strangers hence less of a crime. The privacy, and code of silence surrounding domestic violence in the family context have decriminalized it and spousal battery, thus removing the prohibition against physical violence sanctioned in existing laws. Our mental decriminalization of domestic violence has allowed offenders to perpetrate acts of battery on women with impunity—because the authorities tacitly support, encourage, and reinforce this behavior.

The national outrage at spousal battery in the Nicole Simpson murder is not a new phenomenon. America has been tricked before. Recall Hedda Nussbaum, who in 1988 in New York was paraded on television with blackened eyes, and a severely swollen face from the systematic beatings of her lawyer companion. He, it was revealed, delivered the fatal blows that killed their adopted daughter Lisa. Also, the chief regulator of the Securities and Exchange Commission, who subsequently resigned, self-disclosed that his spousal attacks left his wife with a broken eardrum, bruises, black eyes, and a wrenched neck (Ingrassia and Beck, 1994). The outcry then was boisterous, but it soon subsided having faded to inaction short of any meaningful federal or state legislation to combat the scourge of spousal battery. The collective secrecy surrounding domestic violence in our society makes it difficult to know who among us are spousal batterers. For example, press reports have indicated that O. J. Simpson's lead attorney, Johnnie Cochran, Jr., was a wife abuser. Although the attorney vigorously denied perpetrating verbal abuse or physical violence on his spouse or girlfriend, suspicions linger. Additionally, Kris Jenner, the former wife of O. J. Simpson's business adviser Robert Kardashian, alleges in 1990 divorce papers that she was verbally abused by him repeatedly according to the *New York Post*.

Ingrassia and Beck (1994) aptly pointed out:

> Americans often shrug off domestic violence as if it were no more harmful than Ralph Kramden hoisting a fist and threatening: "One of these days Alice . . . . Pow! Right in the kisser!" But there's nothing funny about it—and the phenomenon of abuse is just as complicated as it is common.

Ralph Kramden's gender-biased humor epitomizes the sentiments and attitudes many men hold about domestic violence. It is trivialized. It is tolerated through humor, and such real-life manifestations as physical beatings, mental, emotional, and psychological abuse.

Domestic Violence Defined

Domestic violence is a term that incorporates physical violence within the family setting, corporal punishment, wife beating, spousal or wife battery, and spousal abuse. Domestic violence encompasses emotional abuse and physical attacks within the family context. Thus, domestic violence affects the entire family constellation including children, parents, grandparents, extended kin of all age groups, and other persons anchored within the family network, who may not be related by blood or marriage.

Spousal Battery Defined

Spousal battery is a chosen pattern of behaving that involves the use of verbal, emotional and psychological abuse, physical and sexual violence to terrorize, intimidate, hurt, victimize, and impose a batterer's will on his spouse, ex-spouse, or girlfriend. Spousal battery is a choice men exercise intentionally and purposefully to resolve conflict and achieve their goals of dominance, and coercive control of women. Spousal battery is a term that incorporates the use of power to maintain gender inequity. Battering is manifested by acts of physical violence, patterns of verbal and psychological abuse, and frequent intimidation. The emotional and physical pain inflicted usually on women and children can be deadly.

The patriarchal and gender-biased system of social relations results in the victimization of women and children. Thus, in its most restricted sense, spousal battery encompasses the broad spectrum of dominance, coercive control, the exercise of power over women, emotional and psychological abuse, and the physical violence perpetrated on a victim and her child or children.

Women Perpetrators

A frequently asked question is: do women use violence on men? Although the numbers are minuscule, women do perpetrate violence on men. Statistics indicate that approximately 95 to 98 percent of the victims of spousal battery are women, and 31 percent of all female homicide victims are killed by their male partners (Browne, 1987; FBI, 1990). *USA Today* (June 20, 1994) estimated that 35 to 45 percent of America's homicides in 1994 were attributed to family violence. Additionally, women murder their husbands or boyfriends in self-defense at a rate seven times more than men who kill their wives or girlfriends while defending themselves. Battered women exhibit less of a propensity to initiate violence against men, but when women behave in a violent manner, it generally is in response to prolonged spousal battery from male partners (Saunders, 1988). There currently are in U.S. prisons 200,000 battered women serving time for defending their lives against their batterers (Kabat, 1994). FBI statistics suggest that women who are convicted of killing their violent partners frequently receive longer prison sentences than men (Browne, 1987).

It is critical to note that spousal battery is not only a male phenomenon. However, the percentage of female perpetrators may not exceed two or five percent of all battery statistics. This notwithstanding, women do perpetrate violence on their partners. Of this two to five percent of women who are violent, a majority has engaged in self-defense. Thus, the percentage of women who initiate spousal abuse is minute. Since men most prevalently perpetrate physical violence, and emotional abuse on women, spousal battery will be addressed from the male batterer's perspective where the woman is victimized. Thus, the pronouns "he" shall be used to designate the male batterer, perpetrator, offender, or abuser, whereas, "she" shall be used for the female victim or survivor. It must be emphasized that this author, and others opposed to violence in general, deplore all forms of domestic violence, spousal abuse and battery whether perpetrated by men, women, or children. The principal goal of this book is to help eliminate spousal abuse, and other forms of domestic violence while simultaneously creating safe environments for women, children, and men.

Legal Definition

The legal definition of domestic violence includes a wide variety of assaults and battery. Sexual assault, sexual battery, or any criminal act that results in physical injury or death to a family member or members, or one who resides permanently or quasi-permanently within a family dwelling, would constitute domestic violence in a legal sense. Family members refer to spouses, former spouses, children who are adopted or related by blood, and individuals embedded in the family constellation, who may or may not be blood relatives. Family members also mean children and their parents; many of whom may or may not have ever cohabited together (Section 741-28, Florida Statues, 1994).

In California, the legal definition of domestic violence includes assault and battery, weapons possession charges, restraining order violations, false imprisonment, forcible entry, and trespassing, which result in misdemeanor crimes. The California Penal Code Section 13700(b) appropriately defines domestic violence as any type of abuse directed against an emancipated minor or adult, who is a spouse, former spouse, or partner in a dating or engagement relationship.

This definition also refers to a cohabitant, former cohabitant, or any individual with whom a perpetrator has had a child. Section 13700(a) of this Penal Code defines abuse as "intentionally and recklessly causing or attempting to cause bodily injury, or placing another person in reasonable apprehension or imminent serious bodily injury, to himself, or another" (Witt, Heath and Gwinn, 1990).

Psychological Definition

Spousal battery is an interpersonal process comprising of the infliction of emotional and physical pain. It includes violent behavior generally accompanied by compulsive verbal and psychological abuse and battery. It is designed to exercise dominance, power, and control predominantly over women. It results in such intrapsychic disturbances as Battered Women Syndrome and Post-Traumatic Stress Disorder, obstruction of psychological growth, anxiety and somatic complaints. Death may also result. Some common concomitants of domestic violence are: anger, drugs and alcohol ingestion, jealousy, a demanding and demeaning attitude, a need to maintain male privilege and status, a callous disregard for a partner's emotional and behavioral independence, insecurity, poor self-worth, low self-image, traumatic childhood experiences, and chronic or acute stress. Although these concomitants do not cause spousal battery, they generally exacerbate a deeply entrenched need to neutralize a woman's power to control her own life. Spousal battery usually emerges from a deeply entrenched need to control and dominate, characterized by a very distinct pattern of assaultive behavior.

The genesis of spousal battery, and other types of domestic violence is rooted in early socialization patterns of parenting and peer group influences. Once the pattern of battery firmly establishes itself in an individual's behavioral repertoire, it involuntarily seeps into adult intimate and social relationships, sibling interactions, peer-group relations, elderly parent and adult child relations, parent-to-child relationships, and other cohabiting arrangements. It is important to emphasize that norms, and institutionalized support reinforce the imbalance of power between women and men, which lead to the batterer's choice to use power and control to maintain this imbalance or gender inequity in his favor. The pattern of assaultive behavior assumes many overt and covert forms, which are manifested through physical violence, intimidation, and threats of violence. The violent acts are perpetrated through use of a variety of means and methods. Some of the most common ones include: an abuser's head, shoulder, teeth, hands, fingers, elbows, feet, or other weapons of varying types.

Magnitude of the Problem

Domestic violence has deleterious effects on women, men, and children. It pervades all racial, socioeconomic, ethnocultural, religious, and age groups in America. Domestic violence occurs in many different forms: spousal battery, spousal verbal and sexual abuse, child abuse, child sexual assault, abuse of parents perpetrated by adult children, family violence occurring between siblings, and elderly abuse. This book focuses primarily on spousal battery, but many of the intervention techniques presented herein can be applied to other types of domestic violence as well. Spousal battery most prevalently refers to the emotional, psychological, verbal, and sexual abuse, and physical violence men perpetrate on their wives and/or girlfriends. As the Duluth Domestic Abuse Intervention Project (1986) illustrates, batterers also use economic abuse, children, isolation, intimidation, coercion and threats, male privilege, minimizing and blaming to exercise power and control over their wives, ex-wives, and girlfriends.

On the average of four times a day, or every sixth hour, a husband, ex-husband, or boyfriend murders a woman in a "crime of passion" precipitated by some intense emotion such as love, jealousy, fear, or in a state of rage or hate (Davis, 1994). The Federal Bureau of Investigation (FBI) indicated in its statistical report that 1,432 women were murdered in 1992 by their husbands, ex-husbands, boyfriends, or live-in-partners (Skorneck, 1994). In 1991 alone, more than ninety women were killed every week in America. Men murdered nine out of these ten women who were killed in 1991 (Senate Judiciary Committee Report, 1992). Former U.S. Surgeon General C. Everett Koop revealed that domestic violence in America is the leading cause of injury to women between ages fifteen and forty-four. One in three American women will be assaulted by an intimate partner in her lifetime warned the American Medical Association in 1992 (Smolowe, 1994). Spousal battery killings occur more frequently than rapes, muggings, and automobile accidents combined (Governor's Task Force on Domestic Violence, 1994). Between four and six million American women are assaulted by their spouse or partner—one every fifteen seconds according to *Newsweek* (July 4, 1994), and the National Coalition Against Domestic Violence (1994).

Domestic Violence Effects on Children

Children are always at risk as potential victims of domestic violence, or the other crimes to which battered women are subjected. Children are most often victims of physical abuse and sexual molestation within the family violence setting. Male children are generally victimized by physical beatings, while girls in the pre-adolescent, and adolescent age groups are sexually assaulted. Children of all ages, whether or not they attempt to rescue the battered parent, are abused in the family. Sixty-two. percent of sons over the age of fourteen were injured when they intervened in an attempt to protect their mothers from physical attacks by abusive male partners. Children who are abused most often have parents who exhibit less positive attitudes, less child-focused behaviors, and less tolerance for normal child development than parents of non-abused youngsters. A preponderance of evidence exists that suggests children victimized by family violence succumb to severe behavioral and emotional problems, particularly when they face their ambivalent feelings for the victimized and victimizing parent. These children perform poorly in school. They suffer multiple behavioral and personality disorders, cognitive dysfunctions, and major adjustment problems as adults (Roy, 1988).

As they are forced to live with family violence, many of these young victims become isolated, alienated, and apathetic. They experience guilt, shame, helplessness, and distrust of adults. They succumb to depression, suicidal thoughts and feelings, homicidal impulses toward the abusing parent, anxiety disorders, and engage in self-mutilation. If warm and supported family members are accessible, or other mature and responsible adults are available to these youngsters of physical abuse and sexual molestation, their subsequent adjustment tends to be enhanced. Many of these abused youngsters remain at risk for continued domestic violence because family violence is repetitious. The abused children learn eventually that they are helpless, and can do little or nothing to extinguish the family violence. As they reach puberty and adolescence, a commonly available option exercised by these victimized youngsters is to run away from home (Bolton, Reich, and Guiterres, 1977). This response is not a panacea. It generally removes the victim from a violent home, but it exposes him or her to such potential victimization as prostitution, drug pushing or use, burglary, shop lifting, or street crime. Early marriage is often an option exercised predominantly by victimized girls (Walker, 1979). Many of these marriages, unfortunately, fail because they are plagued or victimized by the intergenerational cycle of violence. Victims mistakenly believe that the geographical move from the violent family setting, without critically needed counseling, is all that is required for healthy non-violent living.

Some of the effects of domestic violence on children include the following:

Speech problems	Suicidal feelings
Increased sexual activity	Super achiever
Being traumatized	Homicidal tendencies
Truancy	Gender-role confusion
Anxiety and depression	Attacks abusing parents
Violence prone	Nervous disorders
Social withdrawal	Learns to disrespect women
Alcohol and drug abuse	
Sleep disturbances	Antisocial behavior
Running away	Delinquency
Anorexia and bulimia	Conduct disorder
Prostitution	Withdrawal and isolation
Becomes family caretaker	Date rape
Becomes pregnant	Victimization
Poor academic performance	Abuser of others
	Poor coping skills

The emotional, physical, and sexual victimization of individuals leaves indelible psychological scars on its victims, and poses severe long-term behavioral effects. As they become adults, female victims experience interpersonal difficulties relating to men, problems in sexual expression and functioning, and deficits in social skills. Male sexual abuse victims have also reported experiencing difficulties in sexual functioning (Groth, 1979). If a youngster is socialized and raised in a home where domestic violence is a routine occurrence, he or she would have no reference for normality. Thus, unless there is some counseling intervention, the youngster with a family violence background carries this behavior, and belief system into his or her future relationships, with disastrous consequences.

The lives of children are constantly being disrupted by their frequent moves to escape domestic violence. They reportedly lose considerable time out of school. They flee their homes without books and other school supplies. They generally have no money or change of clothing, and are forced to live in the family vehicle when domestic violence centers are full or unavailable. Interviews with children from spousal battery families, who live in domestic violence centers, indicated that, within a twelve-month period, eighty-five percent of these youngsters had temporarily stayed with friends or relatives, and seventy-five percent over the age of fifteen had run away from home at least twice (Roy, 1988). In the U.S., school records are not protected by law, consequently, batterers use these records to locate their partners or kidnap their children. To avert such unpleasant encounters, many battered women keep their children out of school for security reasons (Hoff, 1990; Jaffe, Wolfe, and Wilson, 1990). Children of battered women, who relocate to new school districts, are unable to register in school because they have no birth certificates, immunization records, transfer papers, or other necessary credentials. These were left at home when battered women and their children had to leave hurriedly. Batterers invariably destroyed these school documents as part of their compulsive need to control the battered woman and her children. This has jeopardized, through delay or outright prevention, family members' receipt of welfare aid or housing benefits (Zorza, 1991; Jaffe, Wolfe and Wilson, 1990).

More than 350,000 children are abducted by parents each year in the United States. Fifty-four percent of these abductions are short-term paternal manipulation associated with custody battles. Forty-six percent of these abductions involve taking the children out of state, and concealing their identity and whereabouts. Three out of ten of these abducted children suffer mild to severe mental harm (Finkelhor, Hotaling, and Sedlak, 1990). Over fifty percent of the child abductions are executed by fathers or their representative agents. Men who batter use visitation and other custodial access to their children as the vehicle to intimidate and terrorize victims or retaliate for their separation or divorce. When a battered woman leaves the abusive relationship, there is no guaranteeing her safety and that of her children. Spousal batterers often increase their vigilance, and escalate the violence to reclaim their children, and recapture the battered woman. Statistics indicate that as many as seventy-five percent of medical emergency room visits by battered women occur after they have separated from the violent spousal batterer (Stark and Flitcraft, 1988). Abusive partners manipulate children, and use them as pawns in custody cases to coerce the battered woman into reconciling with them. These coercive incidents occur most frequently during court-ordered visitation (Hart, 1993). Whether it is perpetrated by mothers or fathers, child abuse is likely to decrease after the battered person separates from the violent partner, and finds access to safety services (Giles-Sims, 1985).

Those who claim that children are immune from parental violence are grossly mistaken. In the United States alone, 3.3 million children between the ages of three and seventeen are

exposed to family violence on an annual basis. As a general
rule, seventy percent of the male perpetrators, who batter
their female partners also abuse their children (Bowker,
Arbitell, and McFerron, 1988). As violence against women
escalates in frequency and intensity within the family setting,
children experience a 300-percent increase in physical
violence perpetrated by male batterers (Straus and Gelles,
1990). As discussed in Chapter Four, child witnesses to and
involvement in family or domestic violence are part of their
early socialization, which spawns the intergenerational cycle
of violence, and influences them into becoming adolescent
and adult batterers.

The FBI, women's groups, legislators, law enforcement,
and researchers acknowledge that the data on domestic
violence, especially spousal battery, are underreported. The
monetary and human resource cost of spousal battery is
staggering. The following statistics are a chilling reality of
domestic violence in America.

Medical

- Medical expenditures for domestic violence cost the
  U.S. $3 to $5 billion annually. American business
  debits another $100 billion in lost wages, absenteeism,
  sick leave utilization, and non-productivity (Colorado
  Domestic Violence Coalition, 1991).

- Battered women exhibit psychological disorders
  requiring psychiatric treatment at a rate four to five
  times greater than non-battered women (Koop, 1989).
  Twenty-two to thirty-five percent of those women who
  seek emergency room treatment have identifiable
  symptoms traceable to domestic violence (*Journal of
  the American Medical Association*, 1990).

- Even though one million battered women seek medical
  treatment annually for injuries inflicted by their

husbands, ex-husbands, or boyfriends, medical doctors correctly identified these injuries as caused by spousal battery in only four percent of the time (Stark and Flitcraft, 1982). Families affected by domestic violence visit doctors eight times more often, use emergency room services six times greater, and ingest prescription medication at a rate six times more than the average person (Seattle Domestic Violence Intervention, 1989).

- Violent assaults by a family member pose more serious psychological and physical injury to victims than attacks by a stranger (U.S. Department of Justice, 1980).

Relationships

The negative impact of spousal battery, and other forms of domestic violence on family systems, parent-to-child, and parent-to-parent relationships is enormous as illustrated by these statistics:

- The National Coalition Against Domestic Violence (1994) reported that roughly one of three same gender relationships is abusive, thus showing a higher abuse rate than heterosexuals.

- National victimization surveys indicated that sixteen percent of married couples reported that one or more wife beatings occurred in the first year prior to this survey data collection (Tifft, 1993). Estimates of violent conflicts in marital unions indicate that twenty-seven to fifty percent of these wives are physically assaulted. Unmarried couples who cohabit, and those that enter "remarried families" seem to experience higher levels of domestic violence (Kalmuss and Seltzer, 1986; Carlson, 1987; Arias, Samios, and O'Leary, 1987; Ellis, 1989).

- The National Coalition Against Domestic Violence (1994) reported that fifty percent of all women will be subjected to some form of violence from their partners during marriage. More than one-third of these women experience battery every year.

Women, Adolescents, and Young Children

Women, adolescents, and young children are generally unable to escape the short and long-term effects of domestic violence.

- Roughly fifty percent of all homeless women and children in America are victims of domestic violence, who have fled their abusers. Space limitations in domestic violence centers result in a ratio of two women and their children being refused services for every one accepted. In some urban areas between five and seven women are turned away for every two accepted (Schneider, 1990). After they had received temporary shelter, thirty-one percent of the battered women in New York City resumed residence with their batterers because they were unable to find long-term housing. Yet, in the United States there are three times as many animal shelters as there are domestic violence centers for battered women (Senate Judiciary Committee Hearings, 1990).

- A strong statistical relationship has been established between domestic violence and juvenile justice problems. Adolescents reared with family violence in Massachusetts demonstrated a seventy-four percent more likelihood to commit a crime against another person, are fifty percent more likely to ingest drugs and abuse alcohol, and have a twenty-four percent more chance of committing a sexual assault.

- Women who leave marriages and relationships plagued by domestic violence are seventy-five percent more likely to be injured or killed by their batterers than the ones who stay.

About fifty to seventy-five percent of those men who batter their wives or girlfriends also abuse their children. Children who witness domestic violence succumb to psychological disorders as if they themselves had suffered physical abuse. Child witnesses to domestic violence become prone to perpetuating the intergenerational cycle of domestic violence as they mature. Clinicians report that over sixty-five percent of the men in treatment for battery witnessed paternal abuse of their mothers, and were themselves victims of family violence. Young boys learn in their family structure that violence is an acceptable way to vent their anger, resolve conflict, and control women. Girls are taught to accept violence in silence without protest.

- A woman's standard of living generally dives seventy-three percent after a divorce, while a man experiences an increase of forty-two percent in his standard of living.

- Battering husbands, ex-husbands, boyfriends, or other abusive men account for harassment of seventy-four percent of working women in their place of employment either in person or by telephone (Harlow, 1991). As a direct result of this harassment, twenty percent of these women are terminated from work (Schechter and Gray, 1988).

- Twenty-five percent of such workplace problems as excessive use of medical benefits, low productivity, absenteeism, and employee turnover are attributed to domestic violence (Employee Assistance Providers, 1989).

The Elderly, Immigrant, and Disabled Women

We often overlook such vulnerable groups as the elderly, immigrant, and disabled women in relation to domestic violence. The following statistics are instructive but disheartening:

- Abuse of the elderly is on the rise. Roughly one in twenty-five elderly persons is victimized (Heisler, 1991). The perpetrators of elder abuse may be an adult son or daughter, spouse, ex-spouse, other relatives, or cohabitants. Of those aged persons who experience domestic elderly abuse, thirty-seven percent are neglected, and twenty-six percent are physically attacked. Adult children of the elderly are responsible for thirty percent of the domestic elder abuse (National Aging Resource Center, 1990). As the Florida Governor's Task Force on Domestic Violence observed in its 1994 report, immigrant women, who are battered by their husbands or boyfriends, become "isolated" from the mainstream culture by language and racial barriers. If they originated from oppressive societies, their fear of law enforcement, the judicial system, and U.S. Government is likely to reinforce their need for silence. They are likely to feel dependent on their partners, who use the threat of reporting them to the Immigration and Naturalization Service (INS) for deportation proceedings as leverage to exercise male domination, power, and control. The vulnerability of the disabled woman is exploited by many batterers, who often destroy her prosthetic devices, maliciously dispose of medication, and cancel doctor's appointments, with very few consequences (Florida Governor's Task Force on Domestic Violence, 1994).

Battery of Pregnant Women

Between fifteen and twenty-five percent of America's pregnant women are battered by their husbands or boyfriends many of whom suffer miscarriages and death. The Center for Disease Control and Prevention undertook a study using a representative sample of 1,300 women from four states in the U.S. These women were asked immediately after giving birth whether their husbands or partners had physically abused them during the preceding year. The U.S. states and their statistical percentage of battered pregnant women are as follows: Maine, 3.8; West Virginia, 5.1; Alaska, 6.1; and Oklahoma, 6.9 respectively. Statistical projections based on these numbers suggest that some 240,000 pregnant women are battered annually in the United States (Hilts, 1994). In a research study of 1,200 Caucasian, African-American, and Latina pregnant women, one in six indicated she was physically abused during pregnancy (McFarlane, 1991). Spousal battery of pregnant women, which often results in injury to the fetus, is one of the leading causes of birth defects among newborns. These frightening statistics underscore the large number of pregnant women at risk of serious injury from battery—at a time when they should be experiencing greater bonding with their partners.

These statistics poignantly illustrate the magnitude of domestic violence including its deleterious psychological, emotional, behavioral, and physical effects on women and children. Spousal battery, and other forms of family violence will thrive because the act of battery does not alter or rectify a perpetrator's feeling of insecurity and inadequacy, or his need for dominance, power, and control over a spouse or partner. The unending or repetitious nature of domestic violence is predicated on how early boys learn to use violence against females, a batterer's unwillingness to meet his needs in healthier ways, and society's tolerance for such barbaric treatment of women and children.

Chapter Two, titled "The Spousal Battery Cycle," addresses the emotional and psychological abuse, and physical violence a batterer unleashes on his spouse or girlfriend.

Chapter Two

The Spousal Battery Cycle

A woman can save her life, that of her child or children, and break the intergenerational cycle of domestic violence if she leaves the abuser, and seeks help before, or immediately after the spousal battery begins. After the compulsively chronic pattern of male battery establishes itself, women who leave are at a greater risk of being murdered by their batterer.

V. Michael McKenzie, Ph.D.

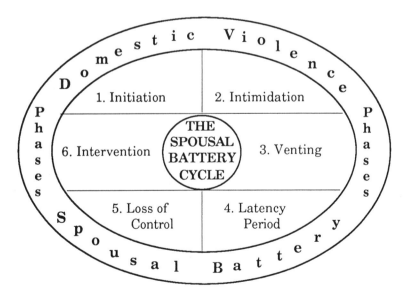

The Spousal Battery Cycle

Spousal battery is learned behavior that is executed purposely and deliberately by a batterer. The batterer's principal goal is to bring about his desired effects of domination, control, and power over a spouse or partner's emotions and behavior. Individuals who engage in wife or spousal abuse exhibit goal-directed behaviors that are easily classified in six distinct phases. These phases include: Phase One— Initiation; Phase Two—Intimidation; Phase Three—Venting; Phase Four—The Latency Period; Phase Five—Loss of Control; and Phase Six—Intervention. Each phase depicts a recurring cycle of behavior and psychological dynamics that are distinctively different qualitatively and quantitatively from the established norms of the previous phase.

Phase one holds the greatest promise of hope for change if the batterer heeds the feedback given about the negative impact of his behavior on the spouse or partner. Also, change is likely if the spouse or partner acts decisively in leaving or seeking professional help before a compulsively chronic pattern of battery establishes itself. When a battered spouse or potentially battered woman takes the definitive action of reporting a violent attack the very first or second time it occurs, the deadly consequences of spousal battery may be permanently forestalled—except, if the victim chooses to enter a new or re-enter the old abusive relationship.

The Spousal Battery Cycle

A. Phase I: Initiation

1. **Dynamics:** Early behavioral signs of spousal battery become apparent generally without any manifestation of the physically violent component. A woman is remarkably intuitive. She quickly

senses the interpersonal tension as her partner becomes unnerved, and prone to violent verbal outbursts in response to frustration, anger, and trivial inconveniences. Apart from the spouse's intuition, his behavioral changes become conspicuous compared to the gentle, sensitive, considerate, and even unperturbed person she has thus far been accustomed to. Whereas, previously, he may have directed his frustration or anger at others or inanimate objects, the husband or boyfriend centers primarily on her behavior. She gets the blunt of his hostility and petulance. He reveals in subtle form some negative personality characteristics previously concealed, exhibited only slightly, or purposely camouflaged.

The potential victim responds with shock, puzzlement, and disbelief. She becomes frightened, tearful, tense, and avoidant. She may regress into prolonged silence, with exterior manifestations of anxiety, confusion, fright, and emotional distance from her partner. She may have hostile thoughts and impulses toward the abuser, and develop shame and remorse in response to her internal hostility.

2. **Batterer's Behavior:** The batterer treats his spouse or partner like a child. Thus parent-child communication patterns begin to dominate their relationship. She is expected to behave like a maid or domestic servant. He unilaterally makes all the significant family decisions, with little or no sensitivity to her needs or feelings. He makes realistic and unrealistic demands, and criticizes her responses whether or not they meet his standards.

In this phase, the batterer engages in loud-talking, yelling, screaming, finger pointing, raising his fist, and invading her interpersonal space. He may stand over the victim, or adjacent to her in such close proximity that her discomfort becomes visible. His compulsive behavior is fraught with rituals that eventually induce anger and/or tears in his partner. She is badgered, followed, or shadowed every place she goes within their home.

3. **Batterer's Aims and Goals:** The flexing of his muscle is part of his psychological warfare designed to confuse, frighten, and weaken a spouse or partner's ego strength. The batterer seeks to ascertain and evaluate how much he can get away with. He tests his partner's resolve. This is his initial attempt to dominate and gain early control over his spouse or girlfriend.

4. **Results:** The spouse or girlfriend experiences a mild to moderate level of confusion or cognitive dissonance in response to the discrepancy between whom he has become compared to who he was. In the mental confusion from this sudden behavioral change, the spouse or partner experiences shock, becomes quiet, and tries to make sense of his new behavior. The spouse questions herself and her partner, and may apologize even when she is guilty of no infraction or misconduct. She may promise to be "good," and pledge full compliance. She may dismiss his behavior as inconsequential, or a transient stress-induced aberration. She may avoid processing what has occurred, and/or minimize her emotional reactions through use of the psychological defense strategy called denial. This phase acts as a powerful hook if the potential

victim is unable to recognize the incipient nature of her mushrooming spousal battery problem.

The battered woman's response is surprise, shock and puzzlement. The sudden strangeness of her partner's behavior leaves her in a state of disbelief. She doubts this is happening, and prefers to think it is her misperception. She gives him the benefit of the doubt. She may either dismiss this initial occurrence as insignificant, or carefully make a mental note and internal registration of this incident for future reference.

B. Phase II: Intimidation

1. **Dynamics:** The batterer gains positive reinforcement from his Phase One pseudo-psychological success, and the spouse or partner's inability or reluctance to challenge the batterer's initial abuse. Peripheral encouragement from same-gender batterers to whom he may have bragged gives him encouragement, and he gains a further psychological sense of entitlement, control, and inspiration. Tension uncomfortably increases, and the spouse or girlfriend desperately, and often unsuccessfully, tries to calm him, and ease the interpersonal tension.

2. **Batterer's Behavior:** Scolding, verbal chastisement, and other parent-child patterns of communication develop between the couple. Verbal abuse accompanied by shoving, pushing, and grabbing dominates his behavioral patterns. A general attitude of disrespect that includes profanity, swearing, blaming, not listening, blatant put-

downs, and caustic negation of the spouse or girlfriend takes hold.

The batterer intensifies her fear by displaying threatening looks, gestures, smashing furniture and household utensils, and destroying her property. He threatens and/or executes some of his threats by hurting her emotionally. He may threaten to make her quit her job, report her to the Welfare Department or Immigration and Naturalization Services (INS), divorce her, or take custody of their children. He becomes unrelenting in his threatening behavior. The introduction of physical force may occur in this phase.

3. **Batterer's Aims and Goals:** His aim is to assert who is in control. He gives vent to his frustrations and negative emotions through his propensity to batter. The batterer intimidates the spouse or partner into submission through escalating tension, fear, and the partner's stressful anticipation of "what is he going to do next?" Anticipatory anxiety has debilitating effects on the spouse or girlfriend, and the batterer exploits this knowledge to its fullest. The early stage of depersonalization and dehumanization generally become evident in this phase.

4. **Results:** The spouse or partner begins to lose her self-confidence, sense of effectiveness, and personhood. She becomes vulnerable to stress-related illness such as depression, anxiety disorders and somatic complaints. Self-doubt, regret, isolation, helplessness and a sense of betrayal generally develop. She may become paralyzed by fear for her safety and that of her children.

Her sleep and appetite are negatively affected. She feels anger, hostility and guilt. The victim experiences a sense of imprisonment, disgust, emotional and economic dependency. The effects of his attacks are evident physically, emotionally, and psychologically.

C. Phase III: Venting

1. **Dynamics:** This phase is characterized by intense emotional abuse, and the beginning of physical violence. Emotional abuse involves verbal attacks by the batterer intended to belittle, degrade, and insult a woman thus causing injury to her self-esteem. Some examples of emotional abuse include:

   - Forcing her to behave in a sub-human fashion that is embarrassing, dehumanizing, degrading, depersonalizing, and humiliating
   - Talking negatively about her to family members and friends in her presence and behind her back
   - Calling her stupid, fat, ugly, incompetent, useless, lazy, and weird
   - Finding fault in her personal appearance, parental and homemaking skills, and blaming her when things go wrong
   - Attacking and belittling her sexual attributes and performance, while embellishing his prowess

   The batterer goes on a rampage of emotional abuse and physical violence. The spouse or partner owns the batterer's rage, and internally centers on her guilt as she struggles unsuccessfully to contain his

explosive abuse. She knows intuitively and
experientially that the rage can increase to lethal
levels, but her determination to fix what she
believes is her fault propels her on. His rage is
fueled by the fear that she will abandon him. They
are now set on a path of destruction—each driven
by an equally pathological logic that defies
intervention.

The victim has seen too many of his outbursts, and
she may experience mood swings, and feelings of
fear and anger. She finds he is less reliable
emotionally because of his surprising behavioral
changes and mood swings. She feels that she is
controlled by his emotions, and acting-out
behaviors. The victim recognizes he displaces his
anger from work and other places onto her. She
becomes deathly worried.

2. **Batterer's Behavior:** The batterer plays mind
    games in which the spouse is belittled and psycho-
    logically undressed. He attacks her character,
    family of origin, and personality deficiencies. He
    makes her beg for money to buy personal items, or
    he confiscates her money if she has a job or other
    sources of income. He uses the children as "go
    between" messengers, and insults her in their
    presence. He controls where she goes, whom she
    talks to, and interacts with. He insults her friends
    and family resulting in their abandonment of her.
    He successfully isolates her from friends and
    family such that his abuse goes unchecked. He
    displays passive aggressive acting-out behaviors
    such as kicking furniture, punching walls,
    mumbling, slamming doors, stamping his feet,
    hissing his teeth, playing the radio or television

loudly, throwing food against the wall, breaking dishes, finding faults, and criticizing his spouse.

His physical abuse includes throwing or tripping her down, twisting her arm, biting, kicking, pulling hair, pushing, shoving, hitting, punching, grabbing, slapping and choking. The batterer comes close to losing control physically and emotionally. Many batterers have reported in therapy that they never intended to injure their spouse or girlfriend. In their vicious attempt to "teach her a lesson," they lose control or become indifferent and callous, afterwards experiencing a tranquil plateau that in its deception does not allow them to gauge the deadly force being exerted.

He may force her to engage in sexual acts against her will, and treat her like a sex object. He may mutilate her sexual organs, and other parts of her body. He may rape her, force her into prostitution, or bring others home to sexually molest her.

3. **Batterer's Aims and Goals:** The physical and emotional abuses are designed to dominate and control a spouse or girlfriend with impunity. Teaching the woman a lesson is synonymous with stripping her of her identity and autonomy. He seeks and achieves her isolation from family and friends so that his battery will not be challenged. The principal goal is to bend and break the spouse psychologically so that she gives up, pledges her complete loyalty, and behaviorally demonstrates full compliance with the batterer's rules. His increased dominance and control get him what he wants, and places him in an exclusive power position over the victim.

4. Results: The emotional abuse and physical violence may continue intermittently, or cease completely. Physical scars and other injuries may be internal; few are ever visible in this phase as the experienced batterer knows he can evade prosecution if such evidence is absent. Many victims exhibit gratitude when the abuse and violence end. Irrespective of the extent of her injuries, a victim often feels lucky for having survived. Her denial prevents her from fully assessing and realizing the seriousness of her injury, which, when coupled with fear, aids her refusal to seek medical care. The injury to her self-esteem is enormous, especially if her children were witnesses or themselves abused. She may be somnolent or in a stupefied state for several days, with stiffness and reduced physical dexterity. He senses victory, so any verbal or physical attacks may be strategically delayed or suspended as he intensifies his aggression.

The batterer may gloat and blame the victim's injuries on her intransigence and stubbornness. He continues to minimize and deny the impact of his violent attacks. His denial and minimization manifest themselves in the following statements he says to her and others: These statements represent his crooked or erroneous thinking (Duluth Domestic Abuse Intervention Project, 1986):

> I lost my temper
> She didn't stop me
> It only happened once in five years
> I didn't really injure her
> I wasn't thinking at the time

She didn't say no
She is a tough girl
She didn't cry for help
I was just kidding
I tried to contain myself
She was wrong and she said sorry
I didn't penetrate her
I'll be careful from now on
I only had sex with my woman
It was really an accident
Things got out of control
It just happened before I realized it
She attacked me first
She knows which buttons to push
I just touched her
She caused the whole thing
It was in self-defense
I am not going to do it again
You know I didn't hurt her

D. Phase IV: The Latency Period

1. **Dynamics:** This is a period of normalcy in which there is a cessation of physical hostilities, verbal and emotional abuse. The relationship and inter-personal climate rapidly shifts to one of cordiality, peaceful co-existence, and pleasure.

2. **Batterer's Behavior:** The batterer expresses affection and becomes contrite. During this phase, the wife beater is cordial, understanding, giving, sensitive, caring, and an empathic listener. He gives of himself lovingly and unselfishly as a husband or boyfriend, parent, and friend. He makes love to her tenderly and passionately, and she enjoys these sexual encounters immensely—

as opposed to the forced sex of recent weeks. She becomes ecstatically hopeful, unable or unwilling to recognize the superficiality and artificiality of this transient moment of false bliss. They cuddle like adolescent lovers, and her gratification nurtures an inner feeling of tranquility and contentment. She is hooked on the feeling of renewed love, and a sense that the cruelty has permanently subsided. All her negative emotions, and other hostile feelings are suppressed as the sense of belonging and intimacy takes control.

The joys of intimacy are not only felt and enjoyed by this couple, they are seen by children, extended kin, and neighbors. This period of tranquility is characterized by professed love, and an attempt to convey genuine remorse. The batterer fears his spouse or girlfriend will leave so hc constantly thrives to undo his violent acts. She relishes the attention and gentleness he lavishes on her, and finds herself easily forgiving his brutality. The victim enjoys a state of relief because the violence has stopped, and the peaceful co-existence is what she has always expected from their relationship. She instantly becomes more compliant, humble, and pleasure centered in her myopic way of holding on to the gratification, tranquility, and peaceful co-existence.

As the batterer vacillates from abuser to gentleman, who showers her with flowers and affection, the victim becomes confused from his dual personality. She experiences ambivalence about leaving, and in effect becomes a willing hostage. The violent abuser, in his instant trans-formation, acquires an attentive, and repentive persona that neutralizes the victim's ability to express her anger, hurt, and pain. She is further estranged from her rage because the mask or facade of this caring father and loving partner impresses her, family members, friends, neighbors, and co-workers. The woman treads delicately for fear she would ruin the peaceful coexistence, but hopeful that the public image of euphoric contentment would replace their private world of violent chaos. She sees his charm and expression of humanity in the public arena, and knows deep within that no one would believe her claims of battery because only she has witnessed the uncontrollable rage in his privately violent attacks (Walker-Hooper, 1981).

At some primitive level the batterer comes to believe, and verbalizes he will not be violent with her again. He unintentionally, and sometimes intentionally bates her, and in her gullible state she allows herself to be bated. She is mesmerized by his attentiveness; charmed, and enthralled by the coziness, respect, and pleasantly secure atmosphere. The battered woman begins to believe he will not be violent with her anymore. She gives up some of her fear and anxiety. The abuser's contrite behavior, this period of respite, and his loving involvement convince her that his violent behavior is rapidly changing. She may become pensive having internalized a guilty sense of responsibility for having precipitated the battery, and her spouse's barbarity.

The battered woman begins to enjoy a sense of calm, a re-experiencing of trust and safety as she lowers her guard or defensive wall including the suspiciousness and hypervigilance. She accepts the false perception that it was really her fault that contributed to his behavior. She relishes the idea that things have returned to normal. She suppresses her memories of the barbarity as she becomes amnesiac. This attitude of hers solidifies his seduction; it places him in a win-win and she in a lose-lose position.

3. **Batterer's Aims and Goals:** The batterer's aim is to manipulate his partner, through a calculated moment of calm and exemplary behavior, into believing meaningful change has occurred. The batterer takes advantage of the momentary respite to re-group while his spouse or girlfriend's defenses are down. The batterer plans and plots his strategy for the next phase of assault and battery.

4. **Results:** The results are an unsuspecting, and somewhat gullible spouse or girlfriend, whose comfortability level with the abusive partner increases, while her fear and resentment decrease. The installation of hope, and increased trust are achieved much to the delight of the batterer. The appearance of authentic cordiality, and a sense of normality prevail. False assurances from the abuser satisfy her need to feel safe. The batterer experiences an egocentric and a pseudo-prideful sense of gratification at his manipulative ability to control his partner, and the prevailing events with precision.

The latency period, with its civility, affection, and close affiliation, makes criminal prosecution of the batterer an impossibility. The victim is unlikely to cooperate with law enforcement because she has become complacent, and is now reluctant to jeopardize a harmonious relationship. As Witt, Heath and Gwinn (1990) so aptly observed:

> A victim-witness advocate who understands the dynamics of the battering cycle can effectively intervene by reminding the victim of similar remorseful periods in the past, predicting a return to the tension building phase, and explaining the likelihood of more frequent and severe injury.

There are many women who do not allow themselves to be deceived or seduced by the batterer in the latency or any other phase of battery. By the time the abuse reaches this phase, some women have emotionally disconnected from the batterer. Others may have left, or on the verge of leaving. The majority, however, tolerate the uncertainty of permanent change, with a paralyzing sense of hope as they stay with the batterer.

Most spousal battery victims, who are preyed upon by their violent partners actively plan and seek assistance from others. Their efforts are seldom successful not only because the predatory behavior of the spousal batterer successfully isolates them from family, friends, and community, but as a result of society's callous and uncaring attitude, and lack of community resources.

E. Phase V: Loss of Control

1. **Dynamics:** This is a behaviorally and emotionally explosive phase characterized by rage, a compulsive need to dominate and control, and intensively cruel battery.

2. **Batterer's Behavior:** As quickly and surprisingly as they had entered the latency period of normality, loss of control descends upon the victim or partner. The spouse or girlfriend may be slapped, kicked, choked, or punched without warning. She may be held against a wall, burned with cigarettes, and raped. These attacks generally occur late at night or in the pre-dawn hours. The beatings are viciously cruel. The slapping, choking, grabbing, and use of weapons threaten her life. She may be struck with an open or closed fist. She may be tripped or pushed, which often results in the victim falling down stairs, or hitting her head on sharp objects.

This is the most dangerous period in domestic violence or spousal battery. Household objects such as knives, pots, pans, a rolling pin, furniture, and electrical appliances are used as weapons. Major injuries are sustained as the batterer loses control, and may be totally dissatisfied with the spouse or girlfriend's promise or gesture of compliance. Some batterers may exhibit a psychotic break with reality, and truly behave like a "mad man."

As the battered woman becomes convinced she is unable to control the batterer's behavior, she exhibits what psychologists have labeled "learned helplessness." She becomes more impotent, and gives up trying to influence positive change in the domestic violence setting. Her anxiety and fear that the batterer will retaliate physically and economically against her, and their children if she leaves increase. Her knowledge that women have been stalked, harassed, and killed by the batterer when they left intensify her fear and justify her staying. Some women, who are severely battered and raped, experience the strongest negative reaction during this phase, and often flee the battering relationship. Many who remain trapped in the violence contemplate, plan, and execute revenge by murdering or attempting to murder the batterer. The victim lives with the horror of victimization through her flashbacks, intrusive thoughts, recollections of the violent abuse, hypervigilant and suspicious behavior, expectation of the increased intensity and frequency of his violence, and lack of trust and safety. An inner sense of rage, hostility, and hate usually triggers her revenge. The victim's willingness to retaliate, and the outrage felt, worry her because they show a capacity or potential for violence she was unaware she had. The victim may blame the batterer for what she has become.

Death could be imminent. Police, the batterer, victim or bystander is generally vulnerable, and could be seriously injured or killed during this phase.

3. **Batterer's Aims and Goals:** The batterer's aim is to regain total control, and spousal submission. He wants to re-experience that pseudo-psychological sense of ego-gratification from his sadistic attacks, and her crying, squirms, pleadings, and the ultimate surrender of a defeated victim.

   He wants to teach a painful lesson of who is in control. He relishes, and seeks, in a bizarre way, the psychological gratification derived from physically beating and humiliating another human being.

4. **Results:** He often gets a behaviorally, psychologically, and an emotionally defeated, and/or physically dismembered human being, who may surrender unconditionally, leave temporarily, or permanently, or be carried out for medical treatment or burial. His emotional abuse and physical violence have totally demolished the victim. Her resurgence can only come from a total disengagement from the batterer.

F. Phase VI: Intervention

1. **Dynamics:** The intervention phase involves an introduction of some third party, who, or third force that interrupts the spousal battery cycle temporarily or permanently—for better or worse. The intervening of a third force is usually welcomed by the victim if she is alive, and resented by the batterer if he is alive.

2. **Batterer's Behavior:** The perpetrator's behavior is characterized by verbal abuse accompanied by uncontrollable physical violence. Continuation of the psychotic-like rage, pent up hostilities, the batterer's accustomed expression of violence, and the last desperate effort to control her fuel his spousal battery at this stage. The use of alcohol and/or drugs exacerbates the conflicts and escalates the violence.

The husband or boyfriend may beat the spouse or partner into a stupor. A cold, callous, and an emotionally unfeeling moment of dominance over a woman in pain, and sometimes near death ensue. He has and shows no remorse. He is unrelenting in his verbal and physical attacks. He is like an animal that has gone berserk. He is uncontrollable.

3. **Batterer's Aims and Goals:** The perpetrator's aim is to transform a spouse or girlfriend into a submissive and compliant non-person, who has relinquished her oppositional stance, and obeys unconditionally. He prefers she be dead than noncompliant.

He seeks to strip the spouse or girlfriend of her identity, self-efficacy, and independence.

His goal is to disarm her psychologically, emotionally, behaviorally, and physically with the appropriate level of physical violence he deems necessary to accomplish his goal.

He thrives to extinguish all oppositional traits, and reduce her capacity and will to resist.

He tries compulsively to achieve these, with no personal, legal, or economic cost to himself. He seeks full and unchallengeable dominance, control, and power over his spouse or girlfriend.

Spousal abuse does not stop even when the batterer idiosyncratically believes he has achieved full dominance, power, and control. There is always a pathological need for greater levels of compliance as the deranged mind knows no limits. Apart from women being prepared to avoid, or effectively extricate themselves from a spousal battery marriage or relationship, prevention, incarceration, however brief, and counseling are some viable options for containing his rage, and changing this lethal violence.

The physical abuse intensifies in this phase. The slapping, pushing, choking, kicking, biting, grabbing, and punching continue without interruption. He may threaten to kill her, or force her to engage in behavior against her will such as prostitution. He may use a knife or point a gun at her that discharges. He may use the family car as a weapon.

Battered women have reportedly engaged in self-blame, and assume responsibility for changing the batterer's behavior believing this would end the violence. Such self-initiated efforts seldom, if ever, have any effect on the batterer's violent behavior. The victim's attempts and failure to change him do not diminish her hopes that he may soon treat her better. Battered women who have been raped and beaten respond with confusion, anger, inner protest, rage, shock, disbelief, anxiety, and a need to take revenge. They also become humble, helpless, and weak in the face of continued abuse.

4. **Results:** A co-worker or friend may intervene directly, or through a telephone call to 911 Emergency Services. Law enforcement may respond resulting in an arrest, or more possibly an urged separation to cool matters off.

   Non-fatal injuries, in which medical treatment is rendered, may alert health care professionals to the presence of spousal battery. Recall that of the one million women who seek medical attention annually for injuries sustained from their husbands, ex-husbands, or boyfriends, doctors correctly diagnose their injuries as domestic violence-related in only four percent of those cases.

In those infrequent cases, medical personnel may initiate a telephone call to law enforcement, who may, depending on jurisdiction and prevailing laws, file charges and execute an arrest.

Concerned family members or neighbors, who are able to penetrate the victim's fortified web of secrecy, and batterer's torturous and unlawful imprisonment of his partner, may be able to assist the women in obtaining medical, residential, legal, and/or psychological help.

Psychological and Behavioral Dynamics of the Battered Woman

Many battered women become prisoners of their homes. They are often paralyzed by the terror of their abuse, and immobilized by the fear for their life and that of their children. Their isolation from family, friends, and other support systems, and the horror of their abuse precipitate incapacitating medical and psychological disorders. To survive the ravages of his onslaught, a battered woman may employ a variety of psychological defenses such as denial or minimization. Some victims come to the sober realization, often too slowly, that they cannot prevent or control a spouse or boyfriend's violent attacks. Like trauma victims, battered women develop perceptual problems, an altered sense of reality, and disturbances of mood. They may suffer from cognitive impairment in which short-term memory may be affected. Their autonomy, self-efficacy, and sense of integrity may disintegrate, and their ability to trust often diminishes.

Self-blame, and self-condemnation may motivate a victim to try harder to save the batterer because her "martyr complex" convinces her that only she understands him. She may become entrenched even deeper in the relationship unaware that her self-identity, self-image, wants, needs, and fate are intertwined with, and defined by his dominance, control, and need for power over her. Her isolation, growing hopelessness, helplessness, and self-destructive propensity take the battered woman closer to her demise as her sphere of options shrinks. The battered woman is encapsulated in her self-delusion that the batterer can change. Her allegiance to, and dependence on him make emotional disentanglement difficult as she rationalizes that her children need a father figure—thus she stays. She is further handicapped by unmarketable skills, and immobilized by a guilt-ridden conscience that disdains abandonment. This mentality seals her fate as the imprisonment continues unabated.

A spouse or girlfriend's resistance is the single most prevalent, and major obstacle to extricating her from the cruel entrapment of spousal battery. She minimizes the frequency and intensity of the violent attacks despite conspicuously clear signs of physical and emotional abuse. She often defends the batterer, and fearfully declines to press charges. The psychological and physical injuries often render her physically numb, apathetic, and afraid that death awaits her for speaking out. The cycle of spousal battery exhausts and dehumanizes a woman such that the resulting physical and psychological weaknesses make it impossible for her to leave, thus resulting in her surrender. The batterer systematically takes control of the woman's psyche as he chips away at her self-esteem and self-image. Her vivid recollections of the torture, and hypervigilance reinforce the fear that keeps her compliant. The battered woman stays in the domestic violence imprisonment because she has lost her self-determination, and believes she deserves such treatment because it is all her fault. When a victim of spousal battery leaves the perpetrator, stalking begins or increases. "Murdered Wife Syndrome" is inevitable if safety services for the victim are not immediately activated.

If the spousal battery victim is killed, the focus shifts from the violence to which she was subjected to a crime of passion, or some equally obnoxious legalistic label that conceals the abuser's barbaric history of violence. Once we pooh pooh or suppress our contempt for domestic violence, we have in essence diminished the significance of spousal battery as a cancerous problem, and relegated it to the annals of secrecy and obscurity. Spousal battery, and other forms of family violence must be kept in the forefront of our consciousness until it is eliminated. Every opportunity must be taken to identify and eradicate the scourge of domestic violence from our midst. The elimination of domestic violence means a significant reduction of a variety of problems, identified in Chapter One, that impair the cognitive, psychological, behavioral, and physical functioning of our children, women, and the batterers themselves.

The Spousal Abuse Rope

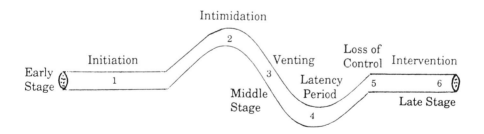

This Diagram Depicts the Stages of Spousal Battery

Chapter Three

The Victim and Victimizer

We can increase a woman's chances of survival beyond the walls of her abusive home, if law enforcement, the judiciary, domestic violence centers, and counselors provide immediate and coordinated services to protect the physical and psychological well-being of a victim and her children.

V. Michael McKenzie, Ph.D.

How Some Women Fight Back

When a battered woman leaves a violent partner, her risk of serious injury or death increases. This increased danger to the victim, known as "separation abuse" is a major obstacle to women leaving abusive relationships. The irony is that many women choose to stay in their violent relationships as a survival strategy weighed against imminent death that may await their departure. This is the strongest negative statement made about the lack of safety services for battered women who flee domestic violence.

Those battered women who stay and endure the abuse, employ a number of untested methods for survival. These strategies range from the legal or illegal, violent or non-violent, and those assisted by family, friends, and the public,

48

or pursued alone. As Mary Ann Dutton (1994) states, "The battered woman may be worn down in her efforts to resist or she may be vibrant, angry, and determined." However, her determination could be short lived and flimsy. The following are those major survival strategies common to most victims:

1. Ignore certain topics and avoid discussions that have generated conflicts and violence in the past.

2. Assume a humbly non-threatening and child-like mode of behavior, and explain her actions when under spousal attack.

3. Use charm, sex, or a new baby to entice or distract him from issues of contention.

4. Request and accept promises that his verbal and physical abuse will stop.

5. Verbally assert herself and physically fight back when under attack.

6. Anticipate battery and take the offensive before he strikes.

7. Threaten to leave and not return.

8. Have an affair for distraction and emotional survival.

9. Take a vacation with or without the batterer.

10. Buy gifts for the batterer.

11. Threaten to call the police and press charges.

12. Threaten to report the battery to a social service agency.

13. Leave home and stay at a hotel, with friends or family until he calms down.

14. Enter a women's domestic violence center, and follow professional recommendations.

15. Call an extended family meeting, pressure him, and extract a promise that he will take a time out when angry.

16. Threaten to file for separation.

17. Threaten to divorce him.

18. Threaten to call his boss.

19. Stay in the violent environment and hope things will improve.

20. Maim or murder the batterer.

Although some of these responses to spousal battery may be constructive and adaptive, most are avoidance measures that placate the batterer and temporarily postpone the inevitable. The following is a list of suggestions for women, and those men who are victims of spousal battery.

- Be aware of what occurs in your environment. Recognize the early signs of abuse: jealousy; envy; impatience; rage; a need for power and control; establishing rules for the victim's behavior, and monitoring compliance; an obsessive compulsive need to know what a woman is doing, where she has been, and with whom; and the unrelenting questioning. Verbal abuse (demeaning remarks, insults, putdowns), and physical force (slapping, pushing, choking) are some early to middle-stage signs of spousal battery.

- Make it unambiguously clear that you will not tolerate spousal battery or any physical violence or emotional abuse. The very first time physical violence is directed against you, exercise your right to live by calling 911 for assistance. Request that a police report be filed, and press for prosecution. Many enlightened judges are making counseling a mandatory part of the batterer's sentence. The moment you decide not to call 911 and press charges, you have in effect affixed your signature to a death warrant. Spousal battery does not spontaneously end, and seldom does a batterer seek help on his own. Many women may find calling 911 and pressing charges to be unthinkable and undoable. They have to be reminded that a batterer behaves the only way he knows, and that his battering behavior requires the learning of new skills for it to be extinguished.

- Another critically important option for a battered woman is making a call to her local women's shelter or crisis counseling hotline. Peer and professionally trained counselors, with clinical experience in spousal abuse, will respond appropriately to your needs. Their support and counseling skills can facilitate your decision-making. Although you may not be ready to make a commitment to therapy, call and explore your options with these professional counselors. Your anonymity and confidentiality will be respected.

- Obtain a restraining or court order of protection to take advantage of its benefits, however meager, and to demonstrate to the batterer that you are serious, and regard domestic violence as a crime punishable by jail.

- Always be prepared that you will be forced to leave your home in a hurry to avoid the deadly consequences of spousal battery. Devise and rehearse an escape plan. As you practice and become proficient in your escape plan, your self-confidence will increase, and you will experience a reduction in anxiety. Have cash easily accessible, an extra set of house and car keys, and a small travel bag with toiletries and clothes. Buy a cellular telephone and keep it fully charged. Break the deadly code of silence; inform your friends and family of the spousal battery. Secure your personal papers, and important documents with close friends or in a safe deposit box. Finally, remove all lethal weapons from your place of abode, and where ever else violent attacks occur.

One of the most courageous acts a battered woman can undertake is to walk away—just leave an abusive marriage or relationship. It is a brave act because it defies death in the face of research findings that suggest a batterer increases his violence when the woman leaves. The realization that he has lost the artificial power, control, and dominance over a woman angers the batterer. He resorts to stalking, harassment, and eventually homicide. A woman increases her chances of survival beyond the violent marriage or relationship, if she presses for prosecution, utilizes domestic counseling services, and leaves without looking back. Just as the drug and alcohol recovery process dictates, the survival of a battered woman may significantly hinge on giving up "people," along with "places," and "things" associated with her spousal battery.

The turning point of change for any battered woman arrives when she can no longer conceal her emotional and physical scars including black eyes, bruises, fractured ribs, broken nose, fingers, hands, toes, or feet. When the victim totally succumbs to the emotional pain, she may then invite others to help. She may not have the necessary finances to sustain herself and her children, but the need to preserve her life may be the driving force for change. She may realize somewhere deep within her psychic that the emotional and physical pain outweighs the monetary rewards and sexual gratification he generates. The fear for her safety may extend to her maternal concern for the children's survival if she is maimed or killed. Men who batter women also emotionally, physically, and sexually abuse their children. Irrespective of the reason, or precipitating factors for her change of mind and willingness to leave, a woman's disentanglement from the lethal grip of her batterer is the sought-after outcome or goal of survival.

Regardless of protective legislation enacted in recent years, increased awareness and knowledge of spousal battery by law enforcement and our judicial system, a proliferation of women's domestic violence centers, and the implementation of intervention programs for batterers, women are no safer today than a decade or two ago. Women are still being pushed, kicked, slapped, bruised, knifed, and murdered. They are being burned by cigarettes, hot liquids, lighted stoves, open flames, and hot coals. Some have had their hands placed in garbage disposals, forced to eat off the floor, while others are made to drink from the toilet. Spousal battery is a scourge of savage fury. It is cruel, barbaric, and a hideously uncivilized act by men who are demons on the inside, but charming, affectionate, cunning, manipulative, giving and lovable on the outside. They lavish their wives or girlfriends with affection, attention, expensive gifts, promises of honor and fidelity— then suddenly, and without warning, they attack—unleashing a barrage of hostile acts on their partners. Battered women seldom talk publicly about the abuse they endure. They are too pained and ashamed to self-disclose the horrors of their existence. They are afraid their self-disclosure would trigger their batterer's cycle of violence. So these women remain silent, tolerate battery, and stay in these lethal relationships.

Why Women Stay in Abusive Relationships?

The most frequently asked questions in spousal battery is why men batter, and why women stay in such violent relationships? Despite its simplistic appearance, the question as to why women live with battery is a complex one. Many women solemnly promise themselves that the first time their mate strikes them they will leave immediately. They quickly find that what they have espoused is not easily actualized. Spousal battery is insidious. It starts slowly, occurs intermittently at first, and by the time an established pattern is discerned, the emotional bond is unbreakable, financial commitments are difficult to renege on, and strong family ties inclusive of children are firmly established. Additionally, when a man hits a woman for the first couple of times, he may apologize profusely, shower her with gifts, attention, and affection, and be visibly shaken and remorseful for his violent act. These, along with his promises never to batter her again, seduce the woman into forgiving and feeling sorry for him. She is conned into giving him a second chance. She does not realize that his apology is designed to remove the unpleasantness (her visible pain or concealed anger and hate) of his domestic abuse, and avoid an in-depth discussion of his behavior. Instead of meaningful atonement and entry into counseling for his wrongdoing, his apology makes the issue undiscussable. What does one do after an apology has been rendered? One automatically closes the issue. Men have manipulatively used apologies to evoke sympathy from a victim, remove the focus from their battery, and its deleterious effects on a partner, and choke off a woman's need and right to express her feelings and disapproval. Thus, any type of negotiation for remedial action, and change itself are unlikely to occur under these circumstances.

The excuses women make for staying in abusive marriages or relationships are as varied as they are real to these battered women. Each woman has her own idiosyncratic rationale for staying in a relationship with a batterer. Some women use religious teachings and spiritual values that condemn separation and divorce as a justification for their continued involvement with a batterer. They point to the marriage vows of "until death do us part," and "for better or for worst" as the anchor that binds them to their marriage or relationship despite its violent character (Ingrassia and Beck, 1994). Others claim they stay for the sake of their children, with little realization of how they foster the intergenerational cycle of battery by exposing their youngsters to this violently dysfunctional mode of domination, control, and power retention through spousal battery. Children are deceived into believing that violence is an appropriate problem solving strategy. It is not.

Women and children are the most impoverished in our society. Thus, their lack of money, and marketable skills are used to rationalize their continued involvement with a batterer. For many women the pain and inner shame prevent them from revealing their beatings. This clandestine mode of existence contributes to their loneliness, isolation, and sense of dehumanization and depersonalization.

The battered woman unrealistically hopes her partner will change and become the charmingly affectionate and caring person he was during their courtship. The emotional turbulence and tranquility that emanate from his simultaneous tenderness and violent outbursts confuse an already ambivalent woman, who is falsely reinforced into believing he will change. Many women are raised with the value system that they can change a wife beater, and internalize the belief that it is their fault that they are beaten. This indoctrination prescribes that if "I" can be a good wife or girlfriend, more pleasant and compliant, less argumentative and stubborn, the beatings will stop. This is a myth. Spousal abusers are cruelly and charmingly manipulative. The battered woman, who is vulnerable and may be psychologically needy, succumbs to the abuser's manipulative charm and need for power, control, and dominance. The self-blame and self-condemnation invalidate herself and perpetuate the dependency on him.

Characteristics of the Victim

Although spousal battery crosses all socioeconomic, religious, age, ethnic and cultural groups, there is no mechanism available to predict who is likely to become an abused person. However, a focus on the social and familial dynamics will give a better understanding of why a battered woman endures the emotional abuse and physical violence of a battle-scarred relationship. Societal norms, cultural values, and personality characteristics influence a woman's reaction to domestic violence including her decision not to leave. Lenore Walker (1979) described some common characteristics of the battered woman. They include:

- She takes responsibility for the abuser's actions.
- She believes the popular myths about battering relationships.
- She has low self-esteem.
- She has strong traditional values about the home, believes in the prescribed female gender-role stereotypes, and strongly subscribes to family unity.
- She experiences intense guilt, but denies her anger and the terror of her battery.
- She exhibits a passive persona, but has the manipulative skills to minimize the frequency and intensity of violence to stay alive.
- She develops adverse psychological and behavioral reactions.
- She uses sex to enhance communication and develop intimacy.
- She firmly believes that no one will rescue her so she must fend for herself.

Many battered women have tried repeatedly and unsuccessfully to get financial assistance and housing. Their sense of being alone, the helpless feeling, and an inability to leave the batterer are reinforced by a reluctance of social agencies to render meaningful assistance (Walker-Hooper, 1981). Most battered women do not control their family finances. The lack of money, and unavailability of housing reinforce the victim's dependency on her abuser. The abuser disapproves of, and obstructs a victim's efforts to find employment. He fears she will be influenced into leaving, hence her isolation, and his maintenance of power and control over her emotions, thoughts, and behavior will be neutralized. The abusive relationship is maintained by the unequal distribution of power, which can be permanently disrupted if she works, earns money, and makes friends. The abusive relationship is maintained by deprivation, intimidation, and isolation. Apart from being stripped of her identity and psychological well-being (self-esteem), the victim loses many of her coping and cognitive skills from prolonged stress. This places her at a disadvantage in the marketplace where she is expected to seek employment, find legal or medical assistance, or manage financial matters. If she manages to leave the abusive relationship, and does not find support and assistance, she is likely to become frustrated, anxious and frightened. These victims' shattered self-confidence and low self-esteem overwhelm them and force them to return. For many, "out-of-fear they seek at last the familiarity of their abusive relationships" (Walker-Hooper, 1981).

Not all battered women are destitute. Some have viable careers, with substantial incomes, but many do not manage or control their earnings. Others who live in superabundant wealth hesitate to leave because of the potential loss of status and monetary goods. Their affluent lifestyle, and ability to frequently travel, as a temporary escape from the batterer, reduce stress and make the abuse somewhat bearable. When children are involved, these battered victims contend that they cannot afford to deny their youngsters the financial, social, cultural, and educational benefits available to them. Their rationalization is simply that tolerance of the intermittent violence has a greater pay-off in the financial reward (Walker-Hooper, 1981).

The following are twenty-one of the major reasons why women stay trapped in abusive relationships:

1. A pro-family stance, and (unhealthy) love for the batterer.
2. The hope and belief battering will stop.
3. Fear of losing custody of her children.
4. Afraid her dependency will cause her to fail when she leaves.
5. The hopeless and helpless feeling that no solutions exist.
6. She feels guilty and remorseful about her mistakes.
7. Self-blame about family violence.
8. Religious beliefs and values.
9. Lack of financial independence.
10. Lack of support from the community (counselors, law enforcement, courts, domestic violence centers, social agencies, etc.).
11. Encouraged by batterer's positive changes.
12. Cultural barriers including language.
13. Fear of partner's revenge including injury or death, or reporting her to the Immigration Department, welfare, etc.
14. Procrastination and indecision.
15. Poor risk-taking, fear of change and the unknown.
16. Fear of being alone without a partner.

17. The need to keep violence a secret, and present a functional exterior.

18. Exhaustion—physically and emotionally drained.

19. The sense of being incapable of managing independently.

20. A sense of personal incompetence (Duluth Domestic Abuse Intervention Project, 1986).

21. The trade-off between tolerance of abuse and the financial rewards of a wealthy comfortable lifestyle.

Who Is at Risk?

The treatment community, academicians, and batterers have focused on the personality traits of women in which the deficiency model is used to demonstrate that battered women lack interpersonal skills and other capabilities. This view holds that the domestic violence victimization of battered spouses is masochistically invited by women whose psychological deficiencies allow them to only choose and attach to dysfunctional men. This blaming the victim approach postulates that women's low self-esteem, passivity, alcohol and other drug use, co-dependency, history of sexual abuse and family violence, "enabler" role, dependency, excessive need for attention, affection, and approval are causal factors in spousal battery. Although these factors increase a woman's risk for battery, this exclusive focus on a cause-effect relationship places blame, and the onus of responsibility for change on the woman. Thus batterers, researchers, therapists, and others who subscribe to this victim-centered explanation are not likely to effect substantive change in domestic violence because they incorrectly focus on the female victim whose causal role is zero.

It is imperative for those male batterers, and that minuscule population of female perpetrators to be held totally
responsible for the physically injurious, and psychologically
damaging forms of violence they inflict on victims. If as a
society, we are unflinching in our condemnation of domestic
violence and battery, and recognize that perpetrators must be
held accountable for their behavior, we are more likely to
intervene uniformly from the educational, law enforcement,
judicial, medical, religious, and clinical perspectives. The
propensity to tolerate excuses from perpetrators such that
they escape the full consequential range of penalties for their
behavior is not unfounded. Psychologists, physicians, social
workers, and mental health counselors "respond to battery on
an isolating case-by-case basis. Often these professionals have
transformed battered women into 'mentally disturbed'
women" (Tifft, 1993). This clinical perspective has failed to
reduce or obliterate spousal battery, generate cohesive interdisciplinary problem solving, or hold perpetrators more
accountable. It has instead further victimized battered
women, and exacerbated the spousal battery problem. Many
law enforcement officers have customarily failed to arrest
assailants while simultaneously discouraging women from
pressing charges. "Similarly, prosecutors have convention-
ally viewed battering 'cases' as inappropriate for criminal
prosecution . . . thereby permitting the partner who battered
to escape the criminalization process" (Tifft, 1993).

It is understood that professionals are at the core of the
domestic violence and spousal battery remediation problem.
Professional intransigence, whether through deficiencies in
training, philosophical differences regarding effective interventions, or membership in the exclusively male gender-
biased clubs that trivialize battery, shall be addressed on an
on-going basis in this book. Suffice it to say that in our gender-
biased social relations, women's needs for safety and em-

powerment are paramount; gender equity in all its spheres is a critical dynamic in preventing and alleviating domestic violence and spousal battery.

John Hopkins University researcher, Jacquelyn Campbell, aptly stated that any woman's risk of spousal battery "has little to do with her and everything to do with whom she marries or dates" (Ingrassia and Beck, 1994). Researchers have begun to empirically identify the risk factors in domestic violence, and most are characteristically male-oriented. For example, men who are young, under-educated, or uneducated, and live in over-crowded poverty stricken areas are more likely to engage in domestic violence and spousal battery. Doctors, lawyers, engineers, accountants and other white-collar men regularly abuse their wives as well. The following are major risk factors for spousal battery and other forms of domestic violence:

- A perpetrator of previous domestic violence or spousal battery acts is identified as the highest risk factor. This is followed by:
- Chronic male unemployment.
- A male who witnessed paternal violence in his family of origin.
- A male who was victimized by family violence as a child.
- A male between the age of 18 and 30 years.
- A male high school drop-out.
- A male who ingests alcohol episodically or regularly.
- A male who uses drugs as infrequently as once a year.
- A male with a blue-collar job if employed.
- A male and female with different religious back-ground.

- A male and female who use corporal punishment, and severe family violence toward their children.

- An unmarried male and female who cohabit.

- An unmarried mother who has not received prenatal care.

- A family income below the poverty line (Tifft, 1993; Ingrassia and Beck, 1994).

Beliefs of Men Who Batter

Although a poor self-image, lack of self-confidence, low self-esteem, an insatiable need for attention, approval, and affection, co-dependency, fear, anxiety, and other personalistic traits may directly contribute to a victim's immobility in an abusive relationship, these factors do not cause domestic violence. Domestic violence, spousal battery, or family abuse emanates from learned behavior. The abusive and assaultive behavior, which is predicated on a gender-biased value system inculcated in early childhood and adolescence, is grounded in a deeply embedded set of beliefs common to all spousal batterers. It is well understood in counseling, psychotherapy, and other clinical methodologies that a person's belief system is the repository for his or her values, thought processes, experiences, expectations, wants, desires, judgments, cultural stereotypes, ethnocentrism, and gender biases. The behavior of a human being is a function of his or her emotions, and thought processes or belief system. In drawing on the Duluth Model of Domestic Abuse Intervention (1986), and self-reports from men and couples who participated in Anger Management and Domestic Violence Intervention groups facilitated by this psychologist, the following beliefs were identified as occurring most commonly among spousal batterers:

BELIEF ONE: Fear, anger, or jealousy cause domestic violence.

Interpretations of this Belief:

- Beating my wife instills fear, and makes her think twice about taking my kids and leaving me.
- I do not worry she will cheat on me because she knows I will kill her.
- Violence is a legitimate response to spousal agitation or provocation.
- Anger makes me lose control and take it out on my wife.
- When I am angry and violent she knows to keep her distance.
- Sometimes she makes me so angry that I can knock some sense into her head—and I do.

BELIEF TWO: Alcohol and/or drugs make me get violent with my wife.

Interpretations of this Belief:

- When I drink and drug long enough I lose it and attack my wife.
- I lose my temper with her easier when I drink and/or use drugs.
- When I am drunk or stoned I don't take her nonsense for too long.
- After ingesting alcohol or drugs, my inhibitions disappear and I act the way I feel.
- It has been dangerously easy to hit and injure my wife after I drank or drugged.

BELIEF THREE: What is the good or benefit in just me changing.

Interpretations of this Belief:

- It is really her fault that I am physically violent with her.
- My wife is the major part of this problem because she provokes, taunts, and gets me going physically.
- There can be no real change if I am the only one required to attend counseling.
- I will change only if my wife shows me she will be different.
- If she doesn't attend counseling sessions with me—I will find no incentive to change.

BELIEF FOUR: Women are just as violent as men.

Interpretations of this Belief:

- Men who are attacked and beaten by women are jailed and sent to counseling—women go free.
- Even though the man and woman both fight, he gets blamed while she is hailed as a victim and sympa-thized with.
- Women manipulate law enforcement, and the judicial system in their favor.
- She is not punished for her violence because she is the woman and mother.
- Even though I start the violence, my wife hits and breaks things as frequently.

BELIEF FIVE: Women are weak so they need to rely and depend on men (who are stronger).

Interpretations of this Belief:

- Men should always be in control because women like it and feel more secure.
- If I do not control her she will try to dominate me.
- If a man is attacked by his spouse he should fight back and win.
- A man is supposed to take charge of a woman.
- Women are dainty and fragile; men should be their protectors.

BELIEF SIX: Breaking things at home is only a release and not spousal abuse.

Interpretations of this Belief:

- A man is still the king in his castle.
- Only wimps allow women to push them around and dictate how things should be.
- Since I buy the things in my house—I can break them as I please.
- When I get crazy and break things, she knows I mean business.
- Breaking things to release the tension is better than hitting her.
- It is my money anyway.
- Sometimes I only want to scare her.

BELIEF SEVEN: If we spank our children like our parents did, today's youth would be more disciplined and respectful.

Interpretations of this Belief:

- Corporal punishment is the only method to instill discipline and respect.
- Spanking is a panacea for the ailments of adolescent misconduct and antisocial behavior.
- The answer to juvenile delinquency is the method of physical discipline practiced by our parents and grandparents.
- The social scientists' idea of putting an end to corporal punishment is responsible for the youth-out-of control (it is not the kids' parents fault).
- If we return to the basics even in this complex world— things will improve.

BELIEF EIGHT: Women's groups instigate our wives into rebelling.

Interpretations of this Belief:

- Women's groups are planting those bad ideas into our wives' head, which are ruining good families.
- A wife's place is in the home taking care of her husband and children.
- If a husband scolds or disciplines his wife she should not disrespect him by fighting back.
- These women judges are empathizing with the wives, and giving the men hell with jail, probation, and group counseling.
- It is a bunch of lesbians who are turning our wives against us.

- The man has no control over his wife and children anymore.
- Those darn shelters are splitting up families when they encourage women to leave their home for a women's domestic violence center.
- No wonder we cannot control today's youth.

BELIEF NINE : Women love being dominated by men.

Interpretations of this Belief:

- She has never said no to me and meant it.
- Most women want to be bossed around and bullied.
- The more you take charge and control her the greater her love and admiration.
- Women have a masochistic side that likes the machismo in a domineering and controlling man.
- My wife loves when I am the boss and make all the decisions.

BELIEF TEN: Domestic Violence is not a big deal—it is just a misunderstanding stemming from a break-down in marital communication.

Interpretations of this Belief:

- If they (people) just respect our privacy and leave us alone we will work it through.
- It is not as bad as it seems.
- Men batter because of their insecurity and jealousy; women stay until it is worked out.
- Men just hit women to stop them from nagging.
- Men do not talk about their emotions such as anger and fear; sometimes they displace these feelings by arguing with and hitting their wife and children.

- Men are good hard-working people, who may hit their spouse out of frustration and intolerance for stress.

BELIEF ELEVEN : A man must know where his wife is at all times and with whom.

Interpretations of this Belief:

- Women cannot be trusted out of your sight.
- Any real man will protect his interest by knowing where she is at all times.
- Women choose the wrong company sometimes so the man has to check on her.
- It still is a man's world, so women have to know their place.
- You have to admit it, a man knows best when it comes to a woman.

If these beliefs represent the thought processes of men, hence their battering behavior, cognitive and behavioral changes become a formidable task. When a man believes and espouses that his violence is precipitated by the imperfection, wrongdoing, mistakes, or other fallible acts committed by his female companion, it implies he is perfect, and has the prerogative to scold or punish her when he deems necessary. This primitive level of thinking is self-generating and idiosyncratic. It does not require a woman's transgression to trigger his reaction because it is internally stimulated originating in his belief system. He uses her behavior as a convenient excuse to justify his indefensible physical violence or battery.

A preponderance of clinical evidence exists in support of our understanding that an individual's prevailing emotional state, and belief system generate a constellation of behaviors that form his or her personality. Men who hold the aforementioned or similar beliefs are predisposed to spousal battery, and other forms of domestic violence because to actualize their beliefs they must unavoidably control the actions or behaviors of women. This predisposition to dominate and control a woman's behavior is often resisted by the woman herself. When such resistance is manifested, the batterer accelerates his force by employing more stringent means to achieve his goal. The intemperate measures he employs to force her compliance are verbal abuse and physical violence.

Although anger, fear, and other emotions do not cause violent behavior, they may add to the frustration he feels and aggravate an already tenuous situation. A predisposition to dominate and control women to achieve one's goals, when met with resistance, provokes tension and escalates conflict, which are usually responded to with physical force as the batterer muscles to achieve his unhealthy goals. Thus, men who hold these or similar beliefs will continue to physically perpetrate violence on their spouse. It is the only choice they make available to themselves, and are willing to use in their pursuit of such counterproductive goals as dominance over and control of women.

It is conveniently and mistakenly believed that being abused as a child is a causal factor in spousal battery, and other forms of domestic or family violence. This is a myth; a falsehood fabricated to lend credence to a batterer's violent behavior. All batterers must be disabused of this self-serving misperception. The pillars of spousal battery are grounded in the gender-biased belief system held by all batterers, and manifested in their attitudes and violent behavior. Childhood abuse places the perpetrator in a high risk category for spousal battery, and other forms of domestic violence; it is not a causal factor. Spousal battery and other types of domestic violence are choices men make, and exercise to dominate and control women.

The need to batter is deeply embedded in a batterer's psyche and behavioral repertoire, which makes spontaneous change or extinction of his violent behavior near to impossible. The tactics and abusive behavior of a batterer are intended to change a partner into a compliant pawn. Batterers depersonalize their victims resulting in a distorted reality, and fragmented self that arrest and eventually retard a woman's emotional growth, which grossly restricts the self-actualization of her human potential (Tifft, 1993). Spousal battery is predicated on the following major beliefs (Hart 1986; Tifft, 1993).

- Individuals who choose to batter have an inherent belief that they are rightfully "entitled" to control their spouse or partner, and that their spouse or partner has an obligation to dutifully comply with all their demands.

- Those who choose to batter believe that violence is a viable option for achieving their goals, and that they do not compromise their moral and ethical values when directing violence against others.

- Persons who choose to batter believe that there are benefits in domestic violence, and they can perpetrate violence against others with impunity.

These beliefs, firmly entrenched in the batterer's personality and behavioral repertoire, are not easily uprooted and modified. The combination of law enforcement, the judiciary, and psychoeducational interventionists working cooperatively will provide the best option for eradicating domestic violence.

Chapter Four

The Making of a Batterer

Spousal battery is learned behavior that originates in the family, and imprints on youngsters as early as age three.

V. Michael McKenzie, Ph.D.

Socialization and Reinforcement

Many parents have consistently denied that their children were present when spousal battery occurred. However, when these youngsters were interviewed, they indicated having heard and witnessed parental violence. They were able to provide detailed descriptions of the emotional abuse and physical battery their parents were unaware they had seen and heard (Jaffe, Wolfe, and Wilson, 1990). Battered women have reported that eighty-seven percent of their children witnessed spousal battery (Walker, 1984).

> Events can be witnessed in many ways, not just by sight. Children may hear their mother's screams and crying; the abuser's threats; sounds of fist hitting flesh, glass breaking, wood splinting, cursing and degrading language. Children also witness the consequences of the abuse after it occurs—their mother's bruises and torn clothes, holes in walls, broken furniture, their mother's tears. They sense the tension in the house, in their mother (National Center on Women and Family Law, 1990).

71

It is unarguably clear, whether parents choose to admit it or not, that children are witnessing the horrible sights and details of domestic violence. It has been demonstrated that child witnessing of family violence is a major risk factor in these youngsters becoming batterers themselves. As was discussed in Chapter Two titled, The Spousal Battery Cycle, domestic violence is pervasive. Perpetrators violently lose control, and women and children are gravely injured. Thus, it is practically impossible to shield children from the effects of domestic violence unless this scourge itself is eliminated. The thrust of this chapter is in its identifying the socializing process that creates the spousal battery problem.

When my daughter Rochelle was four years old, she asked her mother could she go outside to play with her friends. My wife said she could not go because it was close to supper time. Rochelle did not protest this refusal, but came to me instead and posed the same question. I lovingly denied her request, and inquired why she came to me after her mother had said no. She thought intensely for a moment then answered, "because you are the boss." I muffled my laughter long enough to ask her, "why do you think I am the boss?" Without any hesitation Rochelle responded, "because you drive the car and go to work." I was surprised both by how sophisticatedly she conceptualized, and her astute observation even though I knew it was a misperception. I was a full-time student and part-time wage earner, and my wife was the full-time employee. Where would a four-year-old child get such a gender-biased view? She was the only child at this juncture, so sibling influences were absent. Peer group influences were minuscule as she had minimally interacted with her playmates. We could not vouch for the gender neutrality of her day care center, so we admitted this as a possible influence.

After we had factored in the influence of television on the young child's development, we accepted that, and parent-family socializing patterns as part of the major shaping forces in the life of this child. The socialization process is inescapable, and, as we shall discuss, it is at the root or foundation of who we become as adults. The human personality is a product of our genetic predisposition, but disproportionately more a result of how we are raised or socialized in the family setting. When a male child is socialized in a family that devalues and subjugates women, the youngster inculcates gender-biased behaviors, which form the basis for his sexist beliefs that culminate in spousal abuse, and other types of domestic violence. It is critical to emphasize that gender-biased beliefs are the foundation upon which spousal battery is built.

The Batterer's Personality Development

Through observation and imitation, the young child learns and incorporates parental attitudes and attributes including their habits, behavioral patterns, emotions, values, beliefs, strengths, biases, and other weaknesses. Psychologists Nancy Chodorow (1974) and Carol Gilligan (1982) referenced Robert Stoller's (1964) landmark study that suggested gender identity, the basic core of our personality, is "With rare exception firmly and irreversibly established for both sexes by the time a child is around three." Since this identification with the parent or caregiver is the first emotional connection with another human being, the inexperienced child responds as if he or she were the parent. Thus, a youngster who strongly identifies with a parent would feel an inner sense of pride when that caregiver attains a goal, and experiences that achievement as if it were his or her own. In reality, the emotional boundaries for the child are indistinguishable from those of his or her parents or caretakers. The critical point that needs emphasizing is the child's vulnerability to all types of parental influences.

Through the process psychologists have labeled "identification," the child develops a range of behaviors that relate to self-control, morality, self-esteem, his or her conscience, and appropriate gender-role responsibilities. Psychologists have postulated that a youngster's conscience stems from the identification process in which he or she incorporates parental moral standards of conduct that guides his or her behavior in the absence of parental control or supervision. Violation of these learned standards of behavior is apt to generate guilt feelings within the youngster. In his book, *The Productive Personality* (1974), John Gilmore, who drew on Bandura's research, stated:

> The influence of the model on the child's behavior continues even after the model is no longer physically present. Once the model's behavior has been adopted, the child will continue to apply this behavior in situations that he perceives as related to the original modeling situation.

Gilmore cautions, however, that the behavior a youngster exhibits or those aspects with which the child identifies may not necessarily be what the parental model intended. He wrote:

> Children are quite perceptive in identifying with their parents' actual methods of dealing with problems, and parents are sometimes astonished to find behavioral characteristics in their children that they may not even have considered in themselves.

This identification is often seen when a young boy shows special interest in his father's daily activities, expresses a desire to be and grow up like his dad, and wants to demonstrate how much he has learned and benefited from his father's teachings. So when the infant comes into being, he or she needs the continuous attention of a parental figure to provide the basic physiological and psychological needs, and emotional attachment that facilitate the transmission of his or her personality traits. The batterer, as shall be discussed, has the beginnings of his sexist or gender-biased attitudes and behavior in this early attachment and identification period of human development.

After the period of imitation and observational learning has passed, and the youngster becomes cognitively capable of comprehension, the transmission of cultural values, norms, mores, and socioeconomic patterns occurs with rapidity. Here the maturing child learns through interactive relationships with parents, significant other adults (extended family members, godparents, teachers, counselors, religious leaders), and peers, how to participate in his/her social and cultural groups according to all their prescribed rules and regulations. Thus all the factual, occupational, social, sexual, educational, psychosocial, and emotional requirements are imparted to varying degrees.

As the young child builds on the earlier identification learning from his or her parents, the developing youngster grows dependent on relationships with parents and significant others for nurturance and maintenance of his or her self-esteem. As psychologists have emphasized, a significant aspect of socialization is to manage and guide our primitive impulses so that they result in healthy self-esteem. At an unconscious level, the young person quickly learns from models in his or her environment which behaviors are positively or negatively reinforced, and which ones enhance his or her self-esteem. Similarly, these youngsters learn in a haste those behaviors that provide psychic gratification. Many of these behaviors are attributed to gender-biased socialization that they learn from caregivers, and derive gratification through peer and societal reinforcement.

Familial Transmission

The mechanism wherein parental sexist or gender-biased attitudes and behavior are passed on to children begins with the child's identification with parents or caretakers, and continues throughout the socialization process. A young boy's attitudes toward women are patterned after his home environment, where parents appropriately or inappropriately model empathy and respect; how to relate intimately to other human beings; how to acknowledge and express feelings; how to fight constructively and resolve conflict fairly; how to love one's self and express platonic and romantic love to others; and how to work cooperatively. According to John Bradshaw (1988):

> Our families are where we first learn about ourselves. Our core identity comes from the mirroring eyes of our primary caretakers. Our destiny dependent to a large degree on the health of our caretakers.

When caregivers and their social groups are sexist, their gender-biased behaviors are easily transmitted to unsuspecting children whose innocence is intentionally and/or unintentionally exploited. Parents who knowingly or unknowingly communicate subtle or overt messages that women are inferior, or, more directly, treat women at home and elsewhere in a condescending manner, certify to their children that women deserve and should accept such hostile sub-human treatment.

Sexism is intergenerational. It is not difficult to fathom how gender-biased behavior, and its clone racism can be transmitted from one generation to the next through attachment, identification, and the socialization processes. Gender-biased behavior or sexism inflicts pain. It is toxic and pernicious. It deforms masculine and feminine personality. It is a demon of massive proportions, whose subterranean existence cannot be contained so it frequently seeps to the surface with a devastating impact on the lives of women and children. It leaves a gaping wound on its victims' psyche accompanied by indelible psychological scars that excruciatingly remind women of their oppressive siege. It kills vicariously through, for instance, a reduced life expectancy for women. Its lethal fangs kill through spousal battery, and other forms of domestic violence.

The acquisition of sexism or gender-biased behavior is not a magical phenomenon—or an accident. It is learned. No one is born with sexism; it is a maladaptive behavioral pattern inculcated in infancy, childhood, and adolescence through attachment, and identification, and perpetuated by society's tolerance, positive reinforcement, and the pseudo-psychological gratification derived from its practice.

The blueprint for gender differentiation begins before we are born, and as the child comes into the world adults designate blue for boys and pink for girls. These sex role differences accentuated by the gender-specific toys imposed on youngsters embellish the egocentricity of adults and mark the beginning that boys should be men and men be tough and rugged. Gender differentiation regarding a preference for certain games and toys was observed in one to two year-old youngsters. British researchers Pete Smith and Linda Danglish (1977) found that boys of this age group preferred cars and trucks, whereas, girls liked dolls and soft-textured toys. By the time they enter nursery school, boys and girls gravitated to same-gender social groups. This pattern of behavior continues through elementary school where girls show a distinct preference for small groups while boys prefer larger ones. Gender differences in aggression and interpersonal power become evident when children are about two to three years old during which aggressive behavioral patterns emerge and take hold (Hyde, 1984).

Historical Antecedents

A real man conceals his emotions, vulnerabilities, insecurities and weaknesses. He must be decisive. He must always win and never yield an advantage to his opponent. The male must be strong, aggressive, and rational, with the traditional male proviso: earn, provide, and protect. Thus by inference, those protected and provided for are women, who are somehow permanently incapable. As women fight for respect and accessibility, the batterer feeds his compulsive aggression by dominating and exploiting them. He has legacies of experience at dominating because he believes his colonial forefathers implanted the seed to dominate in his genes.

Bred over the centuries to be dominant and aggressive, the Homo Sapient Malc has inculcated gender-dominant traits that operate automatically from unconscious and pre-conscious modes. In his book titled, *Human Aggression* (1970), Anthony Storr states:

> In most of the higher species of animals, including ourselves, the male is habitually more aggressive than the female. The ritualized struggles . . . are a male phenomenon; females do not usually fight each other, either over status or for territory.

Psychologists use aggression in the most restrictive sense to describe verbalizations and overt behavior that are intended and used to hurt other human beings. In survey research findings, men admitted having and exhibiting considerably more aggressive behavior and hostility than women. As Eleanor Maccoby's (1980) research review indicated, "The tendency of males to be more aggressive than females is perhaps the most firmly established sex difference and is a characteristic that transcends culture." It has been demonstrated in every society that men are socially dominant. When individuals assemble in groups, men automatically assume

control and overwhelmingly dominate the leadership responsibilities. In everyday interactions, men more frequently are
gatekeepers and behave as power brokers. They talk faster
and more aggressively, interrupt conversations more often,
and smile less frequently (Mayo and Henley, 1981; Myers,
1986.)

Apart from dominance and aggression, males are seen as
rational and logical, while females are perceived as intuitive,
compliant, and nurturing. Our culture still sanctions a
traditional male role that involves "bread-winner" responsibilities for the economic well-being of the family, protection
from various sources of threat, and the unilateral exercise of
fatherly authority in making decisions. The mother's role is
seen as passive, with the responsibilities to nurture and care
for family members. These male-female roles evolved from an
agrarian society in which protection of one's family, and
mastery of a hostile environment required stamina and the
use of physical skills. The technological era, which
supplanted the industrial revolution and its agrarian
antecedents, placed demands for technical, cognitive, and
interpersonal skills. This changed the perception and reality
of what constituted male and female behavior hence
revolutionized gender-role specialization.

It must be emphasized that individuals from different
ethnocultural and socioeconomic groups may still emphasize
and practice traditional gender-role behavior to varying
degrees. However, and by contrast, in middle- and upper-
class groups there is a decline in the traditional male-female
role differentiation and its division of labor. As men and
women became educated and urbanized, they developed
marketable skills, similar interests, less dependence and
more independence and interdependence, thus neutralizing,
decreasing, or obliterating some gender-role differences. Men
no longer monopolize such professions as engineering,

medicine, law, or space science, although full gender
inclusion is still lacking everywhere. M. Scott Peck's
description is quite relevant in its reinforcement of role
differentiation:

> In marriage there is normally a differentiation of the roles
> of the two spouses, a normally efficient division of labor
> between them. The woman usually does the cooking, house
> cleaning and shopping and cares for the children; the man
> usually maintains employment, handles the finances,
> mows the lawn and makes repairs. Healthy couples
> instinctively will switch roles from time to time. The man
> may cook a meal now and then, spend one day a week with
> the children, clean the house to surprise his wife; the woman
> may get a part-time job, mow the lawn on her husband's
> birthday, or take over the checking account and bill-paying
> for a year. The couple may often think of this role switching
> as a kind of play that adds spice and variety to their
> marriage.

Societal changes that de-emphasized the need for
stamina, brute force, physical skills, and mastery over the
environment, and simultaneously demanded technical,
cognitive, and interpersonal skills, somehow did not tame the
male's dominant and aggressive impulses. Rigidity,
dominance, control, power, manipulation, sexism, territori-
ality, material gain, status, physical force, and an overpowering fatherly or paternal manner form the core of a batterer's
personality.

Batterers are found in all socioeconomic strata. They exist
from the halls of academia through the executive suites and
corridors of Congress to the barrios and ghettos of this nation
where male domination of women is conspicuously common-
place. Some batterers harness legitimate and illegitimate
means to extinguish oppositional forces and perpetuate their
privileged status be they economic tangibles or psychological
intangibles. The batterer's principal goal is to dominate,

control, and homogeneously monopolize the power base such that women are excluded and kept at a subordinate level.

Paternalism and Patronage

In their interactions and transactions with women, particularly the young, impressionable, and career—minded females, batterers seem to inevitably form parental relationship with them, wherein, they quickly establish themselves as mentoring father figures. They emerge as protective, caring, but controlling. As John Molloy (1981) so accurately described:

> Once the parent-child relationship is established, there is no way the power player can be challenged, even on minor issues. These relationships are not necessarily unfriendly, nor do they always involve executive plotting. They are often products of personality types or male-female stereotypes.

Many of these relationships, however, spawn fertile ground for the exploitation of unsuspecting young women—sexual as well as intellectual.

Another characteristic of the batterer is patronization in which he extends unsolicited kindness and assistance as he protects and supports a woman, who may be less equal, equal, or surpass him in a relationship based on knowledge, experi-ence, skill, power, and resource. The *Webster's Dictionary* indicates that to patronize is, "to adopt an air of condescension toward," and patronage is, "kindness done with an air of superiority." John Bradshaw (1988) points out:

> Patronization is a way to feel one-up on another person. Being patronizing leaves the other person feeling shame. The interpersonal transfer of shame through patronization is very subtle. On the surface you seem to be helping the other person through support and encouragement, yet in reality the helping doesn't really help . . . Patronizing is a cover-up for shame, and usually hides contempt and passive-aggressive anger.

The Evaluative and Judgmental Tendency

An effective tactic employed by batterers to maintain gender-distancing and power over women is the evaluative and judgmental attitude. Psychologist Dr. Carl Rogers stated that the major obstacle to mutual interpersonal communication is the natural tendency human beings have to evaluate, judge, approve or disapprove. Novelist John T. Molloy observed:

> Another favorite method for power players to remind subordinates that they are subordinates, is by judging them. They judge their work, the way they dress, how they stand, the kind of restaurant they frequent. They never relinquish their right to judge.

The tendency to judge is common among batterers; it intensifies in emotion-laden situations where deep feelings are attached. In cross-gender interactions meaningful and in-depth communication can only occur when the judgmental tendency is held in abeyance, and active listening is accompanied by empathic understanding. Active listening involves an attitude of genuine concern, caring, and involvement. When a batterer is able to shed his self-absorption and narcissism to listen non-judgmentally and unconditionally to a woman's point of view without evoking his stereotypical attitudes and behavior, effective cross-gender communication is then possible.

In her book, *You Just Don't Understand* (1991), Deborah Tannen suggests that women generally listen when lectured to by men. However, when men are placed in the listening position, they often challenge female speakers by changing the topic and presenting their own agenda. Men fight to control the conversation. They refuse to listen for long periods. In their mind, a listener is in a one-down position, whereas, the speaker is one-up. Men compete to obtain the higher attention status of being the speaker.

Are men able to listen with a posture of positive involvement; try earnestly to sense the feelings behind a woman's expressions; connect to the pain of her exploitation, subjugation, and discontent; and attend to the sorrow of her exclusion? If you could listen uninterruptedly to what she says, and gauge the personal meanings behind her verbal and non-verbal expressions, and sense the tone and emotional flavor of the interaction, then and only then will you have begun the process of meaningful inter-gender communication. Apart from bridging the gender gap and fostering inter-gender cooperation, the development and practice of empathic responses have behavior modification effects on the batterer's personality. As Dr. Carl Rogers observed in his book titled, *On Becoming A Person* (1961):

> It will be of the greatest help to him in altering those very hatreds and fears, and in establishing realistic and harmonious relationships with the very people and situations toward which he has felt hatred and fear.

Perfectionism, Control and Blaming

The batterer is obsessed with perfection and control. Since he sets the standards and requirements of perfection, it is often difficult for others to measure up. Any modification of his rules and standards have a negative backlash as those for whom the accommodations are made are then classified as deficient, inferior, and requiring lower standards. He even sets the standards for feminine beauty (thin, large breasts, proportionately distributed, blond and blue eyed), although, women have increasingly put a halt to his arrogance and presumption. The perfectionist rule is always based on some level or degree of measurement, with his cardinal rule being always be right. According to John Bradshaw:

> Perfectionism is involved whenever we take a negative
> norm or standard and absolutize it. Once absolutized, the
> norm becomes the measure of everything else. We compare
> and judge according to that standard.

The perfectionist stance is another manifestation of his need
to judge. The batterer insists on being right in everything he
does or others do for and with him. His fear and the avoidance
of negative outcomes have become obsessive and compulsive.
His public perfectionist image, which is based on an external
locus of control, has at its core an insecure personality.
Perfectionism denies the fallibility of our humanness.
Associated with his perfectionism, is the batterer's expressed
need to control. He endlessly seeks to monopolize
conversations, manipulate behavior, and control the
expression of feelings. Power comes from the control and
allocation of resources. Since no one but the batterer
measures up, he seeks to maintain full control in all personal
and interpersonal activity.

Since perfection is both irrational and elusive, the batterer
is often faced with disappointment. Instead of giving up the
perfectionist need when unfulfilled expectations arise, he
finds a woman to blame or scapegoat. Blaming is a substitute
for the inability to take responsibility in his dysfunctional
system when loss of control occurs. Blaming maintains the
elusion of perfection. For the batterer, being wrong and
making mistakes are ways of uncovering his insecurity and
revealing the imperfect vulnerable self. To acknowledge a
mistake is tantamount to admitting a flaw and opening
himself to public scrutiny. The batterer detests being scruti-
nized in a public forum where his intellectual weaknesses
and personality vulnerabilities can be examined and exposed,
yet, he relishes demolishing others. He systematically
dismantles his opponents, with little or no hesitation in
publicly shaming and discrediting them. He relishes a good

fight, and uses the evidence from his victories as a self-fulfilling prophecy to demonstrate how inadequate, deficient, and unprepared his opponents are.

Power, Conflict and Domination

In her book titled, *Brain Sex*, co-author Ann Moir (1991) reinforces the point, "Men will make the most extraordinary sacrifices of personal happiness, health, time, friendships, and relationships in the pursuit and maintenance of power, status, and success." Thus, it is evidently clear that the batterer will not voluntarily relinquish his exclusive grip on the reins of power. John Molloy (1981), in his book, *Live for Success*, observed that women are apparently not taught about power during the course of their socialization.

> Most of them had never played team sports in which they had to take charge, interact under pressure, or lead a group, which is where most young men learn to lead and to follow. As a result, the women had little or no practice in exercising authority.

However, Molloy emphasized that after women learned and mastered the fundamentals of power, they exercised it with as much proficiency and savvy as men. Women have an entirely different perspective on power compared to men. "In the female system, power is viewed in much the same way as love. It is limitless, and when it is shared it regenerates and expands. There is no need to hoard it because it only increases when it is given away," observed Ann Wilson Schaef (1985) in her book, *Women's Reality*.

Power-seeking behaviors can be detrimental to one's health. John Jemmott III, a Princeton University psychologist, measured the power and affiliation (the desire to be with people) needs of 195 individuals. Dr. Jemmott found that those individuals who exhibited a higher need for power over affiliation succumbed more readily to depressed immune functions when subjected to stress, whereas, those who placed a higher value on relationships with people had the opposite effect of increased immune functions. The gender difference in value system was further illustrated in a study of 450 entrepreneurial women who completed surveys for Avon Products. A meagre twelve percent of this group rated profits as the principal measure of their success. A sense of self-fulfillment, job challenge, and helping others were respectively rated higher. Women do not define the totality of their achievement and success monetarily as most men do.

Conflict

Confrontation and intimidation are two fighting tactics batterers use to dominate women. "Men like conflict. They relish power struggles in business, sports, and personal relationship," wrote Cris Evatt (1992). Women not only avoid conflictual encounters, many find confrontations quite agonizing and counterproductive. After an altercation, a woman may feel angry, extremely remorseful, or just be demolished. Most men, however, are energized by inter-personal conflict, and may even feel better after a fight because they often do not take it personally. Women are different. "We are anxious about pleasing other people, so we hesitate to speak up about what we think or feel. We qualify our statements with phrases like 'I kinda think' or 'I sorta feel,'" wrote members of the Seattle-King NOW Chapter in their book, *Women, Assert Yourself*. In the work environment men more than women most often confront the boss. Men naturally like to compete, and they relish power struggles as we see in sports, business, and interpersonal relationships.

> Women are intimidated by it. They don't understand the
> game. Women don't challenge because they fear crossing
> the line. If they have a big fight, they think they have to quit.
> Men think they will have to have another fight (Lyn
> Darling, 1990).

Cris Evatt (1992), who drew on David McDonough's
writing in "Men's Health," described "feudus interruptus" as
a fighting strategy most often used by men. Feudus interruptus infuriates women. It involves the uncanny ability men
possess to engage in the most venomous argument, cease all
hostilities for several hours to socialize with friends or
conduct business, with all the charm and attentiveness as if
nothing had happened, then resume the argument much
later exactly at the spot where it was temporarily interrupted.
Jean Baker Miller (1976) in her book, *Toward a New
Psychology of Women*, explained:

> Conflict has been a taboo area for women and for key
> reasons. Women are supposed to be the quintessential
> accommodators, mediators, the adapters, and the soothers.
> Yet conflict is necessary if women are to build for the future.

In his book, *The Road Less Traveled*, M. Scott Peck observed,
"For the truly loving person the act of criticism or
confrontation doesn't come easily, to such a person it is
evident that the act has great potential for arrogance."

Conflict is an interpersonal form of communication that
need not be negative. If individuals battle with clear goals in
mind, and fight fairly, conflict can identify problems,
generate solutions, and provide a better understanding of the
conflicts and ourselves as human beings. Additionally, these
fights allow for the discharge of pent-up resentments, and
when they are done assertively rather than aggressively, a
healthy release of tension results. Numerous studies have
documented that boys are more aggressive than girls, and
they engender higher levels of interpersonal conflict as

opposed to girls' natural affinity for cooperation and harmony. Thus, by the time boys have become men they are proficient in generating conflict. Men are aware that women are not adept at tolerating or managing conflict, thus, conflict has become the major technique men use for winning, subjugating and frustrating women. Men use conflict mercilessly to control and dominate women, and get their way. The following quotations are illustrative of this point. "The games we (men) play in the office, at home, in the world at large, are merely devices to protect the fragility of our own egos" (Michael Korda, 1972).

Domination

The batterer prefers to give rather than receive orders. In the male kingdom, the individual issuing the orders is perceived as superior, whereas, the receiver is viewed as inferior. According to Cris Evatt, "Men actively seek the superior position." In the book, *Talking Power*, Robin Lakoff (1990) wrote, "To utter a direct order is not kind or gentle, since it makes it brutally obvious that the speaker outranks, and has power to control the actions of, the hearer."

To get another human being to take a desired course of action, one can demand, command, coerce, suggest or request. Commands and demands are seen as authoritative, purposeful, power-based, dominant, and regimental or militaristic. Coercion is more manipulative; suggestions and requests are politely neutral with maneuverable room for compliance or refusal. Cris Evatt points out that women's requests tend to be like suggestions because they are often preceded by such "niceties" as "I was wondering if you could?" "Do you mind if I?" "If it's not an inconvenience would you?" As linguist Deborah Tannen (1991) noted, "Girls don't give orders; they express their preferences as suggestions . . . .

Whereas boys say 'Gimme that!' 'Get outta here!' girls say 'Let's do this' and 'How about doing that?' " Since women are noted for showing concern for the feelings of others, they are less comfortable with issuing direct orders for fear of injuring another person's feeling. In the world of work, many assertive women have mastered issuing orders to both men and women. Some have decided that they would prefer to give orders on their own turf and in their own "softer" style.

Men's domination of women has its history in the early developmental years where dominance appears to be associated more with boys' groups than those of girls. Boys exhibit more dominant behavior toward one another than girls. They have also attempted more often than girls to dominate adults as Maccoby and Jacklin (1974) demonstrated in their book, *The Psychology of Sex Differences*. Confrontation and intimidation, that have their origin in early childhood, appear more readily in boys than girls. In male-female relationships, men dominate women through a number of strategies including confrontation and intimidation. These tactics are part of the batterer's arsenal that he employs to subjugate and exploit women. Some women have elected to challenge the batterer with a humanistically superior skill repertoire. Others withdraw choosing instead to associate with those enlightened men and women whose orientation is humanistic, emotional honesty, gender inclusive, and non-manipulative Intergender collaboration.

"We seem to be ready for a greater balance between the games men play and the human equations women factor in," says author Lyn Darling (1990). Women and men have recognized the games men in particular play in conflict-laden relationships. Women are increasingly becoming skilled in the recognition and resolution of interpersonal conflict. Instead of requiring the near impossibility that men change, women are in essence taking responsibility for their own destiny by developing a repertoire of skills they use to constructively confront rather than destructively avoid interpersonal conflict and other counterproductive behavior.

Whether he be educated or undereducated, married or single, divorced or widowed, father or son, husband or brother, young or old, Caucasian or non-Caucasian, heterosexual or homosexual, monocultural or multicultural, religious or atheistic, able or disabled, upper-middle class or lower-class, spousal batterers are the same in their gender-biased beliefs and behavior. Batterers are represented in all social strata, and little evidence is required to see how they attempt to dominate an inordinate number of women. Their deeply entrenched personality characteristics, that transcend race, ethnicity, and socioeconomic status, have developed from parental or caretakers' attachment and identification processes. Parental or caretakers' modeling of gender-biased behaviors takes hold, and peer and other socialization groups provide reinforcement.

The batterer views women as inferior and treats them with covert and overt disdain. When a woman is in an authority position, the batterer is likely to sublimate his resentment and feelings of contempt while in her presence, but gives vent to his true emotions through disparaging remarks behind her back. As a parent, uncle, grandparent, or other designated caregiver, the batterer generally conveys his sexist or gender-biased behavior and attitudes sometimes unconsciously, but often with full cognizance of what he is doing. He stereotypes women in his humor and routine conversations. He is charming and manipulative when he seeks to obtain some favor, including acceptance or copulatory gratification, and holds his judgments and gender-biases temporarily in abeyance to achieve his goals.

As the risk factors suggest, many batterers have been raised in emotionally abusive and physically violent homes. A larger number of men than women in violent relationships witnessed their fathers beating their mothers. The sons of these violent unions, who themselves were usually targets of parental abuse, identified with the parent who abused them and learned that violence is a viable way of resolving their conflicts, or dealing with their emotions. In essence, these violent homes did not provide positive role models for youngsters to communicate their needs, wants, or feelings in a non-aggressive way. These men are yet to experience a real sense of power and control, even over themselves (Walker-Hooper, 1981). Their general sense of powerlessness results in the projection of their insecurities, dislikes, failures, and feelings of inadequacy on others usually women.

Their need for instant gratification, the low frustration tolerance levels, emotional immaturity and dependence, external focusing, and low impulse control make the aggressive behavior of spousal batterers regressively childlike. When the batterer is not violently abusive he is passive and dependent. Even the batterers' request to be nurtured and cared for by his partner is aggressively expressed. Their dependence, which is felt as a weakness, leads to anger that they violently express in the abuse of their partners. The intense jealousy, possessiveness, and fear of desertion are an essential part of the abusive pattern. The victim is never quite able to prove her loyalty and fidelity to the batterer even though he closely monitors her activities (Duluth, 1986; Walker-Hooper, 1981). They eavesdrop on the victim's telephone conversations, read her mail, monitor the odometer readings, check her under-clothes, and even follow her to the bathroom. Some unsuspecting women are seduced by this negative "attention" from their partner. It is only after she experiences the pain and anguish of his pathological jealousy, does she realize he is exercising power and control over her.

Lenore Walker (1979) identified several characteristics common to the spousal batterer. They include:

- Suffers from low self-esteem.
- Frequently engages in sex as an aggressive act to enhance his self-esteem.
- Consumes alcohol and engages in spousal battery to reduce stress.
- Does not believe his violent behavior should have negative consequences.
- Blames others for his abusive behavior.
- Exhibits a dual personality.
- Exhibits pathological jealousy.
- Has the traditional belief in male superiority, and the stereotyped masculine gender role within the family.
- Subscribes to the myths and stereotypes about spousal battery.
- Is preoccupied with weapons.
- Accepts physical violence as an appropriate method of conflict resolution.
- Regularly threatens the safety of or abuses household pets.
- Hunts for the pleasure of killing and not just the sport.

Batterers have been categorized into four different personality types: the Controller, Defender, Approval Seeker, and Incorporator (Elbow, 1977).

Controller   — He sees and uses his partner as an
                    object so that he feels in control

Defender   — He is possessed by hate and love, and
                    is dependent on his partner's
                    forgiveness and acceptance

Approval
Seeker — He seeks from his partner positive reinforcement of his self-image

Incorporator — He sees his spouse or partner as part of himself. He needs to incorporate her ego to feel like a whole person

Elbow suggested that parental messages may account for these batterer's personality types.

Matt-McDonald and Associates (1979) classify abusers into two main categories: "hitters" and "batterers." According to this typology, the hitters assume full responsibility for their violent behavior, and generally warn victims of their escalating anger. Batterers, however, perpetrate more acute and lethal violence at a frequently higher rate. They threaten, intimidate, and terrorize, often refusing to take responsibility for their violent behavior (Saunders, 1992).

Chapter Five

Intergender and Intercultural Training

When a professional communicates with women and culturally different persons free of stereotypes, ethnocentrisms, biases, and judgments, respondents are likely to feel respected, appreciated, and a sense of inclusion rather than engage in the defensiveness of protecting their self-esteem from injury.

V. Michael McKenzie, Ph.D.

Scenario One: Stopped for Speeding

A police officer stopped a female driver because she exceeded the speed limit by fifteen miles. As he approached her car, two young children approximately ages three and six were noticed in the rear seat. The woman avoided eye contact, but bruises on her face were visible. She was disheveled, and appeared rigid. "Howdy ma'am!" the officer greeted. "Do you realize you were speeding?" He asked half expecting a truthful answer. She shrugged her shoulder. "May I see your driver's license, registration, and proof of insurance?" He requested in the professional manner he was taught. "I don't have 'em," she responded, without any attempt to search her pocket book, or dig through the glove compartment.

"This is a text book case," the officer thinks silently. "Just follow your training," he is inwardly directed. "Please step out of the car," he orders as his right hand instinctively finds the handle of his revolver. She complies hesitantly. He frisks her, applies the handcuffs, and escorts her to the patrol car. She sits in the back as he searches her car. The younger child cries hysterically, as the older one unsuccessfully comforts him. The older boy, his cheeks stained with tears, peers through the rear window hungry for a glance of his mother in the squad car. A half-smoked marijuana cigarette, cocaine residue, and drug paraphernalia are found in her car. He holds up the drugs and paraphernalia, then asks her, "are these yours?" She turns her head, and vigorously shakes it to say no before she bursts into tears. "Women are cunning, and crocodile tears could be a sign of guilt." He forces the thought out of his head as quickly as it had entered. He calls for reinforcement. She is read her rights, arrested, and taken downtown for booking.

Questions:

1. Is this an unusual case, or does this happen routinely, frequently or occasionally?

2. Was the arresting officer appropriate, respectful, and professional in his demeanor?

3. Was the police officer's training adequate, not only in executing an arrest safely according to regulations, but in being helpful to the citizen?

4. Would the young children suffer any adverse psychological problems seeing their mother handcuffed and taken to jail?

5. Did the officer miss any vital details that would have resulted in a different outcome for the woman and her children?

6. Would you have arrested this woman?

7. In this anti-drug climate, would issuing her a speeding ticket and letting her go have netted the drugs?

8. Would you have thought or known that this woman is a domestic violence victim who was fleeing the violent home with her children?

9. Would you have made the connection that she had no registration and insurance because the car belonged to her husband, ex-husband, or boyfriend?

10. Would you believe it was his drugs and drug paraphernalia?

11. Are you aware of the high correlation between alcohol ingestion and/or drug abuse and domestic violence?

12. Are you aware that police officers in general, and males in particular often evoke negative reactions including feelings in some victims related to the many times they have called for help, and police either did not come, or did nothing constructive when they came?

13. Should the arresting officer have detected the signs of family violence, and called for the domestic violence unit to respond?

14. Are you still of the opinion, and belief that the arresting officer was appropriate, respectful, professional, and effective?

15. If a doctor medically treats a patient based on a mis-diagnosis, would you as a person, or we as a society call that treatment appropriate, professional, and effective?

16. Would a mis-diagnosis and the accompanying wrong treatment be respectful of a patient?

17. With reference to questions fifteen and sixteen, do you still believe the arresting officer was respectful of the female driver?

18. About the scenario, would you design law enforcement training any different? What would you add? What would you delete? What would you emphasize?

Scenario Two: The Wise Judge

Mary, whose husband was arrested for spousal battery, testified passionately for a non-jail sentence. She used compelling logic to demonstrate how the family could become destitute if his source of income were removed albeit temporarily. She said he was a good father, who drank occasionally, and was drug-free for five years. She claimed this was the first time he had struck her, and it was a result of her provocation. Although she did not become hysterical, her tears evoked compassion and empathy from the court. The broken arm she carried in a cast was the result of a fall several weeks ago from horseback riding, she reported. Even though Mary avoided eye contact with her husband, she openly testified she loved him dearly, and would be lost if he were not around. The judge thanked Mary for her moving testimony.

1. If the judge is gender-biased and/or a batterer himself, would you suspect he would release this batterer with probation, a fine, without a fine, or send him to jail? If the judge were a victim—what might she or he do?

2. Given the spouse's compelling testimony especially the economic argument, would you place the batterer on probation, dismiss the case, remand him to jail, or refer him to counseling?

3. What knowledge or experience would guide your sentence of this batterer?

4. Should the wife's testimony be relied on? If so for what reason?

5. Should the potential financial hardship if the batterer is jailed be a mitigating circumstance in sentencing?

6. If the judge were aware of the dynamics of spousal battery, how might he view the spouse's testimony?

7. Would it have been fair for the judge to lecture the spouse about her collusion or enabling of the batterer's behavior?

8. Is the victim exhibiting signs of the battered women's syndrome?

9. If the batterer were sentenced to jail, but he could serve his time on week-ends, would you consider this a fair or equitable sentence for all parties concerned?

10. Should the batterer not be sentenced to counseling as well?

11. Should counseling be recommended for the spouse too?

12. Given what you know about domestic violence thus far, should counseling be four weeks, eight weeks, three months, six months or longer?

13. What should the judge do if the batterer fails to complete counseling?

14. Is the spouse any safer if the batterer completes or does not complete counseling?

15. Should the spouse and batterer be treated together in the same group, in couples counseling or family therapy?

16. If treated together, would the spouse be able to explore her feelings and self-disclose the violent beatings freely, or would she be intimidated by the batterer?

Before answering question sixteen, read the following excerpt from this author's previous writing:

> This hands-on-component would require law enforcement personnel to make an arrest if probable cause can be established for battery regardless of a victim's willingness or reluctance to press charges. "Ninety-five percent of the time there is a man standing there and a woman bleeding there's no arrest," observed Senator Biden. "The reason there isn't is because the cop turns to the 112-pound woman next to the 220-pound man and says, Are you going to swear out a complaint?" The Senator further emphasized that, "Knowing the man will be out of jail quickly, only to take out his anger on her all over again, this typical beating victim declines to press charges."

Senator Biden's observations capture a significant portion of the intimidation exerted by the batterer, and fear experienced by a victim. This scenario emphasizes the need for training in the dynamics of domestic violence, and the astute level of communication required to better serve the needs of spousal battery victims.

17. Given what you have read about intimidation would the spouse gain the full benefit of counseling if the batterer is present?

18. If the presiding judge were knowledgeable and skilled in recognizing the dynamics of spousal battery, how much credence would he or she attach to the victim's plea for leniency?

Intergender and Intercultural Relations Training

Intergender and intercultural relations involve the verbal and non-verbal behavior that occurs between women and men, and individuals of different ethnic, racial, and cultural background, or persons from the same culture, with a different ethnic or racial identity. Intercultural relations thus denote the communication patterns, interpersonal actions, and accompanying non-verbal behavior that are the context of intergender and intercultural interactions. Research findings have repeatedly indicated that individuals who demonstrate respect and unconditional positive acceptance are more successful in their interpersonal and other behavioral actions with others. Attitudes of gender and cultural superiority, over-simplified and generalized statements about women thwart rapport and other positive communication processes. Negative evaluations and attributions create resentment, misunderstandings, and other communicative barriers when men describe or explain culturally different persons, and women's behavior and motivation from their limited masculine frame of reference and monocultural perspective. Those men who are able to demonstrate empathically that they understand issues and events from a woman's gender and cultural orientation are likely to be more effective in intergender and intercultural relations.

The acquisition of intergender and intercultural communication skills will enable judges, law enforcement personnel, and other professionals to communicate empathically and non-stereotypically with women, and culturally different or minority victims. Any judge or law enforcement person, who was socialized in a monocultural middle-class value system will be unable to fully understand and address the frustrations, deprivations, intimidations, degradations, social conditions, and other experiences of women and minority individuals (McKenzie, 1985). Hence, these professionals' effectiveness in helping is compromised by their cultural encapsulation, and the lack of multicultural communication and intercultural skills. If women, and ethnoculturally different persons are to be correctly understood and properly helped, professionals will have to be effectively trained for intergender and intercultural competence.

> Failure to account for cultural differences inevitably leads to failures in meeting the needs of battered women whose cultural orientation and practices differ from those of the majority culture. While cultural differences must be considered when dealing with battering, they must never be used to deny or excuse the violence, or to perpetuate the myth that certain cultural groups are inherently more violent than others (Governor's Task Force on Domestic Violence, 1994).

Some of the critical goals and expected outcomes in intergender and intercultural relations training are as follows:

Goal I: Assist participants in becoming aware of their own family and educational socialization, monocultural middle-class value system, beliefs, assumptions, and attitudes that are the basis of their ethnic, racial, and cultural stereotypes, and gender-biased behavior.

Goal II: Develop a deeper self-awareness or insight level in which the impact of one's cultural conditioning, stereotypical and ethnocentric behavior on others is understood.

Goal III: Help participants develop a multicultural knowledge repertoire to enhance intergender and intercultural relations (behavior and skills).

Goal IV: Assist participants in developing sensitivity to and respect for the rights of women and minorities including a genuine desire for collaborative sharing.

Goal V: Teach the communication skills of empathic responses, interactive respect, and unconditional positive acceptance.

Goal VI: Extinguish or reduce to its minimum the impulse to pass judgment and attribute unsavory traits to women and minority persons.

Expected Outcomes

1. An acquired ability to detect one's culturally inappropriate, insensitive, and abusive modes of behaving.

2. An awareness of how one's unawareness, and the lack of intergender knowledge and skill contribute to the oppression, subjugation, and exploitation of women.

3. An internalized sense of the cultural influences on one's thoughts, feelings, and behavior including their positive and negative impact on women and minorities.

4. A rich repository of intergender and intercultural knowledge easily accessible for reference and use in problem-solving and rapport-building with women and minority-group persons.

5. A genuine interest in equitable intergender and intercultural relations backed by non-stereotypical and gender-appropriate behavior.

6. An enhanced ability to effectively communicate dignity, respect, positive acceptance, and a valuing of women and ethnoculturally-different individuals.

7. An empathic value system, and an acute sense that gender-biased attributions and evaluations are discriminatory behavior that is offensive, wrong, and hurtful.

8. A natural affinity for gender and ethnocultural inclusion free of patronization, ethnocentrism, and stereotypical behavior.

9. A non-overbearing advocate for gender-equality and non-discriminatory inclusion, with a willingness to challenge unfair conduct and practices.

10. A well-developed intergender and intercultural-skills repertoire for detecting and correcting culturally insensitive, judgmental and evaluative behavior that adversely affects women and minority-group individuals.

In intercultural training, culture has a much broader context than (ethnic and race) ethnoracial differentials. The term culture encompasses the integrated pattern of human behavior inclusive of our beliefs, perceptions, thought patterns, values, customs, communication styles, actions, education, and institutions (Hammond and Yung, 1991; McKenzie, 1985). Intercultural training examines this integrated pattern of behavior to identify those customs, values and beliefs that are stereotypical, ethnocentric, gender-biased, and counterproductive in intercultural, intergender, and other human interactions. A repertoire of gender and culture-appropriate skills are taught for effective communication with women and culturally different or minority persons.

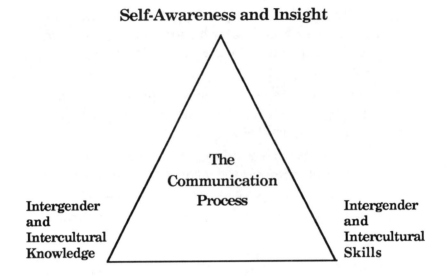

Self-Awareness and Insight

The
Communication
Process

Intergender
and
Intercultural
Knowledge

Intergender
and
Intercultural
Skills

The Tripartite Process of Intergender and
Intercultural Relations Development

Self-Awareness and Insight

Self-Awareness is the hallmark of change; but by itself, change is elusive. Most intergender and intercultural training and development programs focus exclusively on awareness objectives. Their use of values clarification exercises, in which the simplistic dichotomy of "good" and "bad" value judgments are used to underscore cultural differences, fail to provide the knowledge and skills individuals need to apply their awareness. Thus, men may become aware of their racial and gender-discriminatory behavior, but the overpowering sexist attitude, gender-biased value and belief systems remain unaltered leaving these individuals impotent in affecting change. This becomes frustrating for the individual because the awareness magnifies his cultural insensitivity, and the gender-biased problem, but provides no ability to take appropriate action. Thus, it is critical in intergender and intercultural relations training to have a tripartite focus inclusive of self-awareness and insight, multicultural knowledge, and skill development.

The first stage in the tripartite intergender and intercultural training process is self-awareness and insight. Self-awareness begins with a willingness or motivation to pay attention to the internal and external feedback a person gets when interacting with women or culturally different individuals. Often, however, a person's racial and gender-biases may be unconscious, and so deeply layered that he remains unaware of the deleterious effects of his behavior on others. Unless a man recognizes the need to become aware of his unawareness first, and the harmful effects of this unawareness on the lives of others, internal commitment would be lacking, and not much effort will be exerted on learning about himself and gender relations effectiveness.

To be aware of one's behavior, and the negative impact it is having on others, but yet be unable to do something about it is injurious nevertheless. This self-awareness, however, may motivate the individual to seek knowledge and skill. To be unaware of the negative impact of one's behavior on others, and to be unaware of this unawareness is a double-blindness (Argyris, 1976) that can wreak interpersonal havoc in relations with women and minority persons. This double-unawareness or double-blindness results in blaming others, displacing one's anger and other emotions on to victims, stereotyping, or making others the object of one's hostility. Self-awareness helps the professional to understand his or her culturally learned values, beliefs, assumptions, attitudes, and behavior. Insight goes deeper in helping the professional realize that the ethnic jokes, stereotypes, ethnocentrisms, or attitude of cultural superiority are hostilities that come from an insecure person's internal need to dominate and control, hurt and be critical. Internal needs create bodily sensations and discomforts that often cannot be contained, so they find release in a variety of gender and culturally insensitive ways.

Self-awareness and insight allow individuals to understand how their internal forces (thoughts, emotions, and sensations), and cultural conditioning produce their negative evaluations and judgmental tendencies expressed in intergender and intercultural relations. The focus on self-awareness and insight is designed to emphasize learning about one's own cultural assumptions and biases, such that an individual may enter another culture with fewer stereotypes and biases. For professionals or others to be effective when working with women or culturally different persons, they must first understand their value system, and its impact on their own behavior before they can adjust to or even accept other cultural groups. Human beings develop respectful and appropriate responses to women, and minorities through contrast of the familiar and unfamiliar cultural modes with which they come in contact. Self-awareness and insight have little relationship to learning about other cultures directly, but they are an indispensable prerequisite for effective intergender and intercultural relations development. In becoming interculturally effective, we must learn all we can about ourselves in relation to women and minorities. Self-awareness and insight establish for us a secure base for understanding our values, beliefs, judgments, and culturally derived assumptions, and the priority placed on them in our behavior toward women and minorities. Self-awareness and insight are only the beginning of intergender and intercultural relations development. Intergender and intercultural knowledge and skills are the two other components.

Intergender and Intercultural Knowledge

Intergender and intercultural knowledge refer to authentic information about women and culturally different persons learned and used accurately and appropriately. The understanding that stereotypes, gender-biased behavior, and cultural insensitivity obstruct communication, with women and minority individuals is the core of intergender and intercultural knowledge. In domestic violence intervention, the dynamics of spousal battery are a critical part of intergender and intercultural knowledge.

Negative gender-role and racial stereotyping are severely injurious to women and minority-group individuals. When African-Americans or others are categorized as intellectually limited or inferior, this negative racial stereotype results in prejudicial or discriminatory exclusion in which the justification given for the exclusionary act is the generalization recognized by many as false, exaggerated, or fabricated. The apparently positive stereotype that labels Asian-Americans as exceptionally competent in mathematics, and the physical sciences has the negative flip-side in which they are simultaneously seen as weak in verbal and interpersonal skills. This verbal and interpersonal skills deficiency stereotype is grossly inaccurate as applied to Asian-Americans as a group. Although earlier Asian immigrants had problems with language proficiency, today's Asians, most of whom are first, second, or third generation Americans, speak English fluently. Asians are also categorized as passive, dependent and unassertive. This leads to the type of exclusion in which they are often channeled into mechanical and engineering type jobs to the exclusion of people-oriented careers.

When Latinos are stereotyped as highly emotional, shiftless, unpunctual, and instant gratifiers, this allows for the stereotypical categorization of this cultural group as irresponsible and unreliable for certain jobs or career positions emphasizing dependability. These stereotypes are pervasive, and they leave little or no room for individual differences. Thus, when Asians, Blacks, Latinos, Native Americans, or other minorities disprove the stereotypes and excel, they are then patronizingly described as a first, maverick, an aberration, unique, different, or exceptional.

Ethnocentric individuals are those who judge other cultures as bad, wrong, inferior, or primitive only because the culturally different individuals are just that—different. Studies have shown that people who are prone to ethnocentrism are generally interculturally intolerant and insensitive. Ethnocentrism and stereotyping are related in that their negativity toward, and contempt for culturally different persons and women coincide with the hostile verbiage, and objectionable labeling practiced by the ethnocentric individual, whose goal is to hold women and minority persons at a distance thus justifying their exclusion from full participation.

Intergender and Intercultural Knowledge

- Knowledge of communication processes
- Knowledge of how to help victims
- Dynamics of spousal battery

Carl Rogers warned that one of the barriers to communication may be the human tendency to be judgmental. One's inclination to be evaluative may stem from a rather ethnocentric self-centeredness that precludes taking the other person's gender and cultural perspective into account. Researcher Barnlund (1975) has suggested that human defenses result not from the "expectation of differences," but from the "expectation of criticisms." When communication is fraught with criticism, individuals erect protective barriers to prevent injury to their self-esteem. Psychologist Broome (1981) recognized that cultural differences are threatening to many individuals; the familiar and similar nurture trust, whereas, the dissimilar and unfamiliar arouse alarm and discomfort. While gender and cultural similarities play an important role in the effective delivery and receipt of messages, intercultural communication, which includes varied cultural backgrounds and linguistic codes, may be a potential source for distorted messages and mutual misunderstanding.

A non-judgmental attitude and open-mindedness are facilitating attitudes in communication; they communicate respect and empathy for individuals generally, but especially for those who differ culturally noted educators McDaniels (1974), and Millar and Millar (1976). Communication expert Gibb (1961) suggested that non-evaluative communication requires that communicants present their feelings without requiring that the receiver change attitudes or behavior. Rogers' clinical experience, and Gibb's research findings suggest that a non-judgmental, non-evaluative communicative style and atmosphere promote understanding between individuals. When such a style is used and an atmosphere created, professional and victim share and respond empathically, reaching out for each other's ideas instead of defending their own. When human beings are aware that they will be accepted, respected, and liked unconditionally, then the likelihood is increased that they will freely and deeply explore a wider range of gender and cultural differences. According to communication researcher Kleinjans (1972), the intercultural communicator:

- Sees a human being first and a representative of culture second
- Is aware of the value of his or her culture and that of the other person
- Has control over his or her visceral reactions to women and culturally different individuals

- Believes that human beings are basically good and have integrity
- Is a secure person with no discomforts about being different from other human beings

Behavioral scientist Harris (1973) described four characteristics necessary for effective intercultural communication. They include:

a. Strong personality

b. Competent teacher

c. Comfortable intercultural interactant

d. Competence in interpersonal relations

Researcher Ruben (1976) thoroughly reviewed the literature on communication competence in the United States and listed seven communicative behavior characteristics he found to be important in intercultural effectiveness. They are:

a. Showing respect

b. Having an interactive posture

c. Empathy

d. Role behavior

e. Orientation to knowledge

f. Interactive management, and

g. Tolerance for ambiguity

Communication experts were among the first to point out that our ability to communicate in any language requires developing and mastering a non-verbal repertoire of skills. The importance of intercultural contact cannot be over-emphasized. The correct use and interpretation of gestures and body movements of any culture require knowledge of the verbal contexts in which they originate. Researchers Kendon (1967; 1970; 1977), and Nielsen (1964) noted that British and

North American Whites have behavioral patterns that involve considerably more looking than listening when involved in communication. African-Americans, who live in Northern areas of the United States, look more while speaking and less while listening. La France and Mayo (1976) observed that the amount of looking (eye contact) did not differ for Blacks and Whites it differed in the time they chose to look. Psychologist F. Erickson (1976) noted that eye contact while listening is a practice valued by Whites whereas it is optional for Blacks and other minority groups.

French and Von Raffler Engel (1973) found that during story recitation, white students paused before conjunctions and at the beginning of clauses. African-Americans, however, paused at points where significant changes in pitch occurred often in the middle of clauses. Whites considered these ungrammatical because they occurred unexpectedly. Bishop reported those communication styles that match one's cultural group are received very positively, while dissimilar styles are assessed negatively. This researcher also found that Whites were more receptive to Blacks who spoke standard English than those who did not. In a study involving community college counselors and students, Erickson (1976) reported that the more counselors and students were alike in linguistic styles and social identity, the greater the likelihood of a smooth interview. Communication barriers are erected when a person deliberately or inadvertently fails to recognize and respect cultural variations in styles and patterns of verbal and non-verbal communication. As Dillard (1983) asserted, exclusive attention to an individual's verbalizations is, in essence, a refusal to recognize the whole person and his or her culture or gender.

The Dynamics of Domestic Violence

A minority of judges are educated in the dynamics of domestic violence: the six phases of spousal abuse; batterers' manipulations; minimization; denial and other defense mechanisms; the deleterious effects of family violence on victims including children; the revolving-door justice; victims' restitution or lack thereof; batterers' lack of accountability; batterers' inability to take responsibility for their crimes; and the rehabilitation process. Judges who understand, and are versed in domestic violence dynamics are more likely to render decisions that protect women and children, and provide the legal and clinical services necessary for their well-being. These enlightened and skilled judges are also more likely to appropriately punish perpetrators while making rehabilitation an available option for these batterers. Training can unquestionably make a meaningful difference in the way victims and perpetrators are treated, and the overall outcome of domestic violence cases. The Florida Governor's Task Force on Domestic Violence (1994) made a number of valid recommendations, twelve of which are presented herein because of their relevance to this topic.

- Judges must become educated in applicable laws relating to domestic violence, including use of expert testimony on "Battered Women's Syndrome," the dynamics of family violence and its continuing effects on children.

- Judges must become educated about the harmful effects of gender bias and prejudice in court proceedings and judicial decisions.

- Judges should ensure that court-certified interpreters, including those required under the American Disabilities Act, be available as needed in all court proceedings. If any party needs an interpreter, the court should make certain that a court-certified interpreter is available before proceeding. Neither party nor their children should be asked to translate for the court.

- Judges must specifically structure all orders of protection in domestic violence cases in concise language, and must base the issuance of such orders on whether domestic violence has occurred or whether there is reasonable fear that it may be imminent.

- Judges must monitor compliance with all civil court orders, including structured visitation schedules, no-contact clauses, custody, support, removal from residence, and batterer's program participation.

- Judges should set bail at first appearance, if appropriate, with the warning that there be no victim contact and that all special conditions of pre-trial release be imposed and monitored. Judges should ensure that reasonable efforts are made to notify the victim before the defendant's release. (The court should instruct the victim to provide notification of any change of address.)

- Courts should make appropriate counseling referrals, order psychological evaluations, and consider electronic monitoring to increase victim safety.

- Courts, state attorneys, and the Department of Corrections should coordinate their efforts to ensure that all mechanisms for monitoring pretrial release defendants are instituted, and that they are consistent with the intended purpose.

- The Bar Association should:

    a) ensure that continuing legal education on domestic violence topics is available for all members of the Bar; and incorporate domestic violence issues into interdisciplinary continuing legal education seminars such as immigration and public interest law.

  b) should require that training in domestic violence
      be mandatory for attorney certification in family
      and criminal law.

• Law schools in Florida and throughout the nation
  should create a task force to develop teaching materi -
  als to deal with relevant domestic violence topics to be
  included in family law, criminal law, torts and
  contracts courses. This task force should also provide
  guidance for integrating domestic violence education
  into other appropriate areas of the curricula.

In conclusion, intergender and intercultural relations
development is the process wherein individuals learn to
identify their culturally learned assumptions, biases, beliefs,
values, attitudes, opinions, stereotypes, ethnocentrisms,
prejudices, and evaluative and judgmental behavior. These
unexamined cultural influences can produce negative interpersonal effects that impede intercultural communication
and cohesiveness. However, when this cultural conditioning
is examined, understood, and behaviorally modified, it
becomes facilitative in intergender and intercultural
relations. Intercultural ignorance is a fertile bed for interpersonal conflict when working with battered women and
multicultural groups. Thus, intercultural relations
development is predicated on the assumption that human
beings can co-exist harmoniously only after they have consciously and authentically examined their underlying gender
and cultural values and biases, like themselves and their
cultural identity, understand that others are different
wherein different does not mean bad or inferior, and invest in
a mutually interdependent exchange and sharing on the
emotional, psychological, and intellectual levels.

Chapters Six and Seven will address the skills component
of intergender and intercultural relations when working
specifically with spousal battery victims.

Chapter Six

Law Enforcement and the Judiciary

> If a battered woman were assured of security
> services, and that the community would be available
> to her unconditionally, and without judgment or
> condemnation, she may without hesitation, extricate
> herself from her domestic violence purgatory.
>
> V. Michael McKenzie, Ph.D.

Can Spousal Battery Be Stopped?

Fifteen U.S. states have laws requiring arrests in
domestic violence cases, but law enforcement compliance
with these laws is exceedingly low. New York City, for
instance, has a 1979 family law that requires mandatory
arrest, and the filing of an official report on all domestic calls
received. However, a 1993 study reported that of the 200,000
annual calls received, official reports were filed in only thirty
percent or 60,000 of these cases. More shocking was the reve-
lation that arrests for that year were executed in only seven
percent or 14,000 of these 200,000 cases (Ingrassia and Beck,
1994). It is popularly reported and believed that police officers,
factoring out the usual exceptions to this practice, detest
getting involved in domestic violence complaints because
these disputes have unpredictably dangerous outcomes.

Sometimes a seemingly innocuous call to 911 pertaining to a family quarrel may result in a cordial reception for the cops; other times this routine call may involve warring parties who attack the peacemakers. Thus, standard law enforcement procedures have evolved that require two police officers to respond to domestic violence complaints. Additionally, police officers are warned to be hypervigilant, and maintain eye contact with the antagonists at all times. Irrespective of how dangerous spousal conflicts have become, many law enforcement agencies do not consider domestic violence to be criminal activity.

Law enforcement representatives have argued that their officers should be allowed to exercise individual judgment, and not arrest everyone indiscriminately in response to domestic violence complaints. They have insisted unilaterally that minor family violence cases risk being tossed out of court for lack of credible evidence. They further assert that if mandates are placed on law enforcement agencies, the same procedures should be followed by court officers. Prosecutors have vociferously disagreed, and voiced their own frustration. The "he said she said," or "he did she did" testimonies result in inordinate court delays, and reported postponement of cases that could not prevail in court in their original form. The prospects of a batterer being incarcerated on the testimony of his spouse or girlfriend is unsettling, and in some cases traumatic for the intimidated woman—so she acquiesces and the batterer walks unpunished (Ingrassia and Beck, 1994). Nationally or universally standardized procedures shall be discussed later in this chapter as a solution to the intimidated woman, whose failure to press charges, and testify account for low prosecution rates in domestic violence.

However, effective domestic violence intervention is similar to crisis counseling. The intervention strategy or remedial action must be immediate, thorough, and decisive because an individual's needs change immediately after the crisis has abated. When a woman calls 911, it is because she is in an acute crisis, imminent danger, scared, and wants immediate help. Even the slightest shift in focus that does not address her immediate needs risks being experienced by her as irrelevant, unempathic, and unsatisfying. Thus, any mention of dispositions, subpoenas, court appearances, testimony, or prosecution may not be in the victim's immediate sphere of consciousness, hence she is likely to be an uncooperative and reluctant participant.

Unless the law enforcement community, and judicial system overhaul their policies and procedures, their positive impact on domestic violence will be minuscule or negligible. Irrespective of sound, laws such as the New York City Family Violence Law, and well-intentioned professionals, spousal battery continues to psychologically impair, maim, and kill its predominantly female victim population. It must be emphasized that many law enforcement agencies around this nation have begun to make relevant changes in their management of domestic violence, and particularly spousal abuse cases. However, a large segment of the law enforcement community, and our anachronistic judicial system have remained complacent thus irrelevant and ineffective in responding to the needs of battered women.

Both the judiciary, and law enforcement personnel can begin their transformation to effective intervention systems by exerting their influence in reshaping the misperception that spousal battery is not a criminal act. This is not an easy goal to attain because of personal values, professional training, and years of practice. Additionally, it would be impractical and unfair to expect such a spontaneous transformation without some training for the judicial and law enforcement personnel, and other professionals.

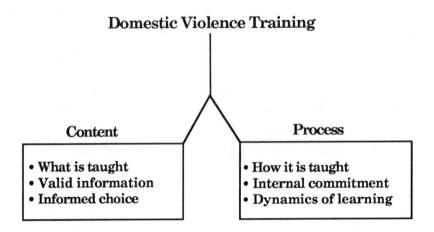

Besides its appropriate goals and objectives, any meaningful training must attend to:

   a. Valid information,

   b. Informed choice free of coercion

   c. Internal commitment to that choice (Argyris, 1976).

Valid information means that the training information
being disseminated is not contrived, falsified, purely opinion-
based, but the most accurate, current, and research-oriented
data available. Free and informed choice addresses one's
involvement in the training processes or other activity, free of
coercion or any type of supervisory force. It also involves
knowledge of why the training is required, and how the skills
gained are going to be used. Internal commitment to that
choice is a psychological dynamic of personally accepting,
internally committing, and taking ownership for one's motivation, active participation, participatory satisfaction in the
learning process, and learning outcome. When valid information, informed choice, free of coercion, and internal
commitment to that choice are present, the learning

processes and pedagogical outcomes are greatly enhanced and more beneficial.

Domestic violence training for law enforcement, judicial, and medical personnel should have goals and objectives that reflect a non-stereotypical, non-racial, and gender-impartial agenda. It must be a unified and coordinated approach, which conveys the poignant message that domestic violence is inherently wrong, a crime against persons, and an unlawful act that will not be tolerated. The myth that spousal abuse, or family violence is more prevalent among some ethnocultural groups should be debunked. Domestic violence pervades all socioeconomic, ethnoracial, ethnocultural, religious, and age groups regardless of sexual orientation or national origin. The domestic violence curriculum must be broad in its scope to include the following:

- The pervasive nature and pernicious effects of domestic violence including its varied manifestations as depicted in the legal and psychological definitions.

- The effects of domestic violence on children, the elderly, immigrant and culturally different women and men, and persons with disabilities.

- The statistical profile of domestic violence including fatalities and non-fatalities.

- The human resource and financial costs, with emphasis on the excessive utilization of medical benefits; workforce effects such as absenteeism, low productivity, and staggering turnover.

- The physiological and psychological effects of spousal battery and family violence on women and children.

- An ability to recognize the signs and symptoms of domestic violence including the victim's denial, and batterer's manipulation and minimization of his brutal acts.

- Intervention strategies: police officers' safety, effective arrest, and referral for medical treatment including psychological counseling.
- Pro-arrest policies and procedures that facilitate rather than impede problem amelioration, with monitoring mechanisms to gauge precinct compliance.
- Cultural norms and society's attitudes that perpetuate rather than extinguish domestic violence.

Domestic violence training for the law enforcement community can easily be incorporated in the basic recruit curriculum. In-service, and annual training will be able to address the domestic violence competency training needs of those police officers already on the force. Domestic violence training for law enforcement personnel must be mandated on an annual basis. Besides those already mentioned, the goals and objectives of this training would incorporate the following:

- Explore the feasibility of a Domestic Violence Unit (DVU), or Family Violence Officer (FVO) in each precinct around the nation.
- Develop procedures for collecting evidence, documenting findings, and preparing written reports in domestic violence cases.
- Develop a protocol for responding to the needs of children, criminal justice options for victims, and services available to victims and batterers (legal rights and remedies).
- Develop an in-depth familiarity with laws and statues pertaining to domestic violence including misdemeanor and felony arrests, and injunctions for protection (acquisition and enforcement).
- Prepare for dissemination a brochure listing comprehensive services such as: victim rights; options in the

legal process; course of action if a victim is threatened, stalked, or battered again; information on Women's Domestic Violence Centers and treatment facilities.

- Law enforcement agencies should receive current and quality material on domestic violence including spousal battery from the criminal justice system.

Law enforcement intervention, with victims of domestic violence including spousal battery, requires specialized knowledge and skills acquired through training. Police intervention is normally the first critical step in managing domestic violence problems. Training will ensure that these officers intervene in a more deliberate and purposeful manner rather than a trial and error approach. Victims of family violence, especially immediately after a battery attack, may be disheveled and disoriented, thus confused, inarticulate, agitated, and seemingly uncooperative. Trained law enforcement officers who have some specialization in domestic violence would be able to recognize the signs or symptoms of domestic violence. This would allow them to engage in crisis management, and draw on their knowledge of the community domestic violence and medical center resources to triage the victim so that she gets the appropriate assistance. The domestic violence training would allow the police officer to apprise the victim of her legal rights, and give her the appropriate literature.

Role of the Judiciary

Judges, prosecutors, and defense attorneys, indeed the entire judicial system, can play a revolutionary role in deterring family violence in America. Judges are already empowered through their office to make a meaningful contribution to the elimination of domestic violence in our nation. A judge's ability to be a potent change agent in the scourge of domestic violence must begin with his or her unbiased and objective view of women as equal partners in the domestic and professional ranks of our human family. Gender biased beliefs and their accompanying behavior, in which one's philosophical stance encompasses the subjugation and exploitation of women, serve only to inflate the male ego, trample the aspirations of women, and deny them due process. Before a judge, and other officers of the court can become impartial allies in the fight against domestic violence, they must undergo training on two levels: (1) Intrapersonal Awareness, and (2) the Dynamics of Domestic Violence.

Law enforcement officers are usually the first to arrive at a domestic violence dispute. Their legal authority to stop violence, and armed presence are feared by many batterers who recognize police force as greater than themselves. Police officers must act decisively and quickly; avoid overreacting and exceeding their authority. Their presence, which can increase or decrease anxiety, must be used to deescalate tension. They must present a calm and helpful demeanor, and caring attitude. The paramount concern should be protection of the victim. This must be followed by restoring peace, giving legal and other referral information, and facilitating emergency transportation.

Law enforcement contact with the victim and batterer can be used not only to ascertain, and respond to the victim's needs, but also in gathering prosecutory evidence. When law enforcement officers arrest a batterer or offender of family violence, this single act sends a poignant message to the victim, perpetrator, and public that domestic violence, family violence, and spousal battery are offensive, intolerable, and a serious crime (Governor's Task Force on Domestic Violence, 1994). Behavioral changes at the individual level, and procedural changes at the systemic level in the law enforcement community must begin with the awareness of, and followed by the practice that:

- Spousal battery is not the fault of a woman, who is victimized by a batterer.

- Spousal battery, and other forms of domestic violence should not be treated as victimless crimes, and rationalized as endemic of our social pathology hence warranting secondary or tertiary consideration and intervention.

- The variability from under-reaction to overreaction in law enforcement officers' response to spousal battery, because the warring parties may or may not be acquainted, is unprofessional, unethical, counter-productive, and perpetuates inequitable intervention.

- To rationalize and explain the causal factors of battery, and other forms of domestic violence may be unintentionally biased, and not within the purview of law enforcement personnel. This lecturing behavior even if competently and elegantly displayed, trivializes spousal battery, and other forms of domestic violence, and negates the victim.

- The decision to arrest a batterer should not be based on the public or private occurrence of an offense, nor any idiosyncratic belief that prosecution will not materialize. Arrest must be based on evidence and legitimate complaints.

The following module is designed to provide a guideline for law enforcement officers, who are assigned temporarily or permanently to investigate domestic violence incidents (Training Key #246, 1976).

1. Receiving and Documenting Complaints

The Emergency Telephone Operator must quickly, but accurately get all pertinent information from a caller, who may or may not be the victim. Keep the telephone line open. Ascertain the type and extent of injuries; types of weapons used, presence and ages of children, location and description of the batterer. Listen for statements emphasized and/or repeated by victims, and monitor background noises. If possible, have the victim meet law enforcement officers outside the home or apartment.

2. Arriving at the Scene

Safety and caution are paramount. Police officers must approach the domestic violence scene from the most advantageous point that offers them maximum protection. Keen observation, and a preemptive view inside the dwelling permit a quick assessment of human activity before announcing police presence. This "plain view" approach helps establish probable cause that a crime was committed. Be vigilant, and mindful of your partner(s) presence.

3. Meeting the Combatants

A pleasant demeanor, followed by a warm introduction of who you are, and stating why you are there have proven to be effective. If entry is denied, respectfully and calmly explain you cannot leave without assurance and confirmation that no one is under attack or hurt. If access to the home is denied a second time, forced entry is appropriate if there is reasonable belief that a victim or someone else is in danger. Forced entry must conform to standard police operating procedures. Some examples that would justify forced entry include: Cries from children, adult cries for help, home in disarray with evidence of a struggle, displayed weapons, eye witnesses.

4. Taking Control

Quickly but safely locate all occupants. Gauge the extent of injuries, and determine if weapons are present. Separate the warring parties, and interview them one at a time while your partner functions as a guard. If only two individuals are involved, separate and simultaneous interviews can be conducted. The kitchen should be avoided because it is the repository for weapons. Witnesses should be removed to legitimize their status for future hearings. When alleged batterers begin to make incriminating statements, Police Officers must apprise them of their legal rights:

5. Interviewing and Protecting the Victim

The immediate cessation of violence, protection of the victim from further battery, and provision of first aid are paramount. Chapter Six addresses in detail the dynamics of spousal battery. However, the victim's injuries are usually internal: abdominal areas, breasts, genitalia, portion of head covered by hair, and the back. Pregnant women generally sustain injuries in the stomach area. Call for medical assistance without delay.

Some victims become incoherent and irrational, with a stupefied appearance. Whether or not the psychological shock is obvious, do not leave the victim unattended. The traumatic experience may have damaged the victim's self-esteem, shut her down psychologically, and render her speechless and helpless. Given this psychological profile, the police officer can be most effective showing concern for the physical and psychological well-being of a victim. All victims are culturally different and unique in their personality composition. Do not assume you know what she is feeling, thinking, or will express. Be empathic, but give her the freedom to express her emotions. Crisis causes confusion and incoherence. Listen with patience, a non-judgmental tone, and caring posture. Give realistic, but not false assurances.

The officer's verbal and non-verbal messages can build rapport or destroy her self-confidence. Appropriate eye contact, not staring, a warm smile, and encouragers such as slight nods and friendly head and arm gestures reinforce camaraderie and support. Similarly, non-judgmental and neutral responses such as "yes," or "I see what you mean," and "please, tell me some more," encourage communication and a positive feeling about the helping officers.

6. Interviewing Witnesses

Interviews with witnesses should be sooner rather than later. Impress on witnesses the seriousness and unlawful nature of the alleged abuse and/or battery, and ask for their full cooperation. Evaluate the inconsistencies in what is presented. Cross-check to validate and invalidate information given. Solicit from neighbors or family members prior domestic violence incidents. Compile domestic violence history. Secure physical evidence, note in writing relevant observations, and take photographs of evidentiary data.

7. Interviewing the Perpetrator

Interviewing the perpetrator on the scene to ascertain facts or elicit incriminating evidence is permissible. Non-verbal body language such as shifting in his seat may provide clues to further pursue the interrogation. Angry outbursts, and changing the subject of discussion may be leads to intensify the questioning. If the alleged perpetrator becomes a criminal suspect, he must be advised of his legal rights.

Law Enforcement and the Judiciary Flow Chart

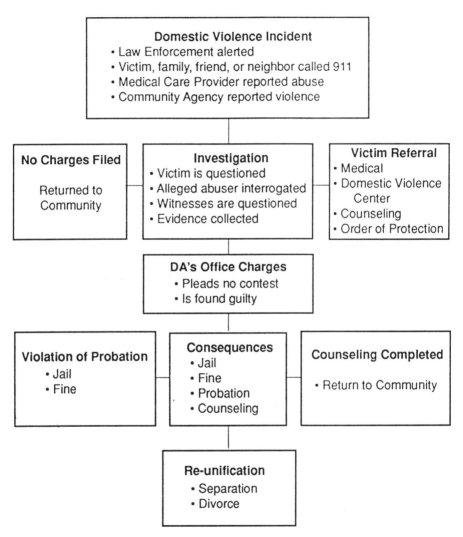

Domestic Violence Incident
- Law Enforcement alerted
- Victim, family, friend, or neighbor called 911
- Medical Care Provider reported abuse
- Community Agency reported violence

No Charges Filed

Returned to Community

Investigation
- Victim is questioned
- Alleged abuser interrogated
- Witnesses are questioned
- Evidence collected

Victim Referral
- Medical
- Domestic Violence Center
- Counseling
- Order of Protection

DA's Office Charges
- Pleads no contest
- Is found guilty

Violation of Probation
- Jail
- Fine

Consequences
- Jail
- Fine
- Probation
- Counseling

Counseling Completed

- Return to Community

Re-unification
- Separation
- Divorce

This Law Enforcement and Judiciary Flow Chart depicts possible consequences when a domestic violence incident is reported.

8. Gathering Evidence

Established procedures for gathering evidentiary data must be strictly followed: victim accounts, medical reports, photographs, and crime scene data must be secured. Proof that the battery suspect was advised of his rights is crucial and must be securely preserved.

9. Arresting the Alleged Perpetrator

When a police officer is not present during the assault, as in misdemeanor cases, the victim has to secure an arrest warrant. When substantial physical and circumstantial evidence exists, as in felony cases, an investigator can ensure that an arrest is executed for probable cause without any need for a victim's cooperation (Training Key #246, 1976; Walker-Hooper, 1981).

Law enforcement has a vital role in the cessation and elimination of domestic violence in our society. There is no substitute for competently trained, gender neutral, and interculturally skilled police officers responding to domestic violence complaints. If an officer has self-awareness and insight, intergender and intercultural knowledge, and the requisite skills for intergender and intercultural communication, he or she will be effective intervening in domestic violence disputes.

Chapter Seven

Treating the Victim's Physical Wounds

When health care providers realize that they are treating many domestic violence victims, their condemnation of this family violence will close another escape route for the perpetrator, and his world of spousal battery would have shrunk significantly.

V. Michael McKenzie, Ph.D.

Training of Medical Personnel

Recall that of the one million battered women who seek medical treatment annually for injuries inflicted by their husbands, ex-husbands, or boyfriends, medical doctors correctly identify these injuries as caused by domestic violence in only four percent of the time. This dismal statistic is a major supporting factor for the training of health care providers. A health care provider is any individual, who is licensed, or unlicensed but works under supervision to provide patient care. This may include: physician, psychologist, nurse, social worker, nurse practitioner, practical nurse, nurse's aide, dentist, podiatrist, chiropractor, medical assistant, physician assistant, medical technologist, medical

or dental technician, laboratory assistant, mental health
counselor, or other mental health providers.

The following goals and objectives are critical in the
delivery of appropriate and effective medical assistance to
victims of domestic violence. The delivery of health care
services must always be grounded in respectful and dignified
treatment of all domestic violence victims.

Goals and Objectives:

- Recognize that domestic violence has deleterious
  effects on women, children, men, the elderly and
  disabled, immigrant persons, and individuals from
  same gender relationships.

- Recognize the acute, chronic, and pervasive nature of
  domestic violence including its long-term effects on
  victims, their family, and the community.

- Recognize the enormous mental health, medical,
  occupational, and other monetary costs incurred
  through spousal battery and other forms of domestic
  violence.

- Develop insight and remedial strategies for removing
  the barriers that inhibit effective communication and
  intervention between battered persons and health care
  providers.

- Develop screening or diagnostic techniques to identify
  psychological, behavioral, and physical signs and
  symptoms of domestic violence, and incorporate them
  into routine medical examinations.

- Develop and use appropriate intergender and intercultural interview and intervention methods, and assess
  clients' level of risk for future family violence.

- Treat domestic violence victims with respect, dignity,
  and sensitivity being mindful to prevent clients from

further victimization by the very system from which they seek relief.

- Respect client confidentiality, promote autonomy and self-direction, report and document domestic violence as required by clinical protocol pursuant to federal and state laws.

- Inform clients when the law mandates the reporting of suspected or substantiated domestic violence.

- Promote and encourage professional development, education, and training for health care colleagues in the diagnosis, treatment, reporting, and interpersonal support for clients victimized by domestic violence.

- Utilize domestic violence centers, counselors, and other referral resources in the interdisciplinary management of domestic violence cases.

Interpersonal Barriers in Treatment

Women in general, and culturally different individuals in particular, must overcome many barriers before they are able or willing to receive medical treatment for family violence. Health care providers must themselves make many cognitive and behavioral adjustments before they are acceptable to, and capable of working effectively with domestic violence victims. An understanding of spousal battery dynamics, and knowledge of intercultural and intergender communication can facilitate the screening and treatment processes. The ethnic and cultural or ethnocultural values and beliefs, religious norms, and family sanctions may prevent a domestic violence victim from revealing or self-disclosing her abuse to strangers. The victim may be uncooperative because she fears the batterer's threats of retaliation may be realized. The victim's love for and loyalty to the perpetrator, including her fear of being alone, may reinforce her silence. Her economic dependence, belief in two-parent families, and concern that the batterer may harm himself or be unable to function, may force her to conceal the abuse.

Unless the health care provider is aware of these barriers, understands their origin, and has the skill to work through them, he or she will be ineffective. As we have discussed, the victim's belief that the batterer will change, her guilt and self-blame, the denial and minimization of his violence act collectively to keep her from disclosing the abuse. She may be ashamed and humiliated, unable to recognize an abusive relationship because it is all her fault, and visualize the injuries as minor or unrelated to domestic violence. Some lesbians and gay men may conceal the abuse so as not to disclose their homosexuality (Santa Clara County Domestic Violence Council and Board of Supervisors, 1994).

The health care provider may have his or her biases. These biases undoubtedly impede the appropriate response, and create frustration for victim and practitioner alike. A common bias is the misperception that domestic violence occurs only in the lower classes, thus a middle or upper class patient is not at risk. A related assumption indicates that if the patient does not voluntarily disclose abuse none has occurred. This reluctance to ask a patient about abuse often springs from the health professional's fear of offending the victim, or a sense that it is not the role of the Health Care Provider to question or intervene. The health professional may be reluctant to become involved in such a personal or intimate matter, or feel unprepared to grapple with the complex dynamics of domestic violence. Some personalistic pitfalls that impede the process include blaming the victim, showing one's frustration, questioning why she stays, and expressing disbelief because the perpetrator appears to be incapable of such cruelty. If the health professional displays discomfort, or is judgmental and insensitive when same-gender abuse, or violence by women perpetrators is revealed, the patient may feel disrespected, angry, ashamed, slighted, and will most likely refuse further assistance.

How does one avoid disrespect, insensitivity, and other personalistic pitfalls that can impede the interview, hence prevent a victim from receiving appropriately helpful assistance? Since the clinical interview is critical in getting data upon which treatment will be based, the professional must be circumspect in attitude and professional decorum. Negative evaluation, subtle condemnation, judgmental and disapproving attitudes, and offensive questions are to be avoided. Do not ask the following questions: Why do you stay in that relationship? Aren't you tired or had enough? What do you get out of the violence? What did you do for him to hit you? What could you do to avoid or minimize the abuse? An evaluative interview must be free of attacks, insults, innuendoes, and the types of condescending attitudes reminiscent of the domestic violence relationship the victim experiences. The following questions are consistent with an appropriate diagnostic interview in domestic violence screening.

Domestic Violence Diagnostic Interview

1. Do you feel anxious or afraid around your partner or generally in regard to your relationship?
2. Are you ever threatened by your spouse or partner?
3. Are you verbally, emotionally, or psychologically abused in your relationship?
4. Are you insulted, disrespected, called names or treated badly in your relationship?
5. Have you been pushed, slapped, punched, kicked, had your hair pulled, hit or battered in the last six months? Or anytime before that?
6. Has your partner ever destroyed items you own?

7. Has your partner ever threatened or abused you?

8. Has your partner ever threatened or abused your kids?

9. Has your partner abused any pets?

10. Has your partner forced you into any sexual act against your will?

11. Has your partner belittled you sexually?

12. What happens when you and your partner have a conflict or disagreement?

13. Has your partner ever stopped you from leaving your home or apartment, or being with your family and friends?

14. Has your partner forced you to quit school or work?

15. Has your partner harassed you at work in person or over the telephone?

16. Does your partner check your underwear, inquire where you were and with whom? Or accuse you of unfaithfulness?

17. Is your partner jealous and possessive?

When a patient is seen or examined, the health professional must be vigilant to the signs that indicate domestic violence has occurred. These signs can be placed in the verbal and non-verbal behavioral categories.

Behavioral Signs

- Tremors, sighing, crying, blank stares
- Fidgeting, anxiety, nervous or inappropriate laughter or smiles
- Anger, fear, a defensive posture
- Poor or lack of eye contact, fearful eye contact

- Denies violence or minimizes the seriousness of her injury
- An overly attentive, aggressive, defensive, impatient, or uncooperative partner
- Reluctant and uncomfortable speaking in the presence of a spouse or partner
- Partner offers explanation for injury

Verbal Signs

- The victim talks about helplessness, or a friend who was abused.
- The victim focuses on a partner's anger or loss of temper.
- The victim answers in the affirmative to one or more of the Domestic Violence Diagnostic Interview questions.
- The victim asks for information on or a referral to a Domestic Violence Center.

Miscellaneous Signs

- A victim's repeated need for medical services for an injury to the same limb or organ, particularly psycho-somatic complaints.
- Complaints such as anxiety, depression, fatigue, nightmares, insomnia, sleep disorders, headaches, memory problems, difficulty concentrating, suicidal feelings or gestures, marital conflict, sexual difficul-ties, abdominal and gastrointestinal complaints, Post-Traumatic Stress Disorder (PTSD) complaints as described in Chapter Nine.

The Physical Examination

In performing a physical examination, the physician must be attentive, and ensure that all techniques used aim for an accurate medical diagnosis of domestic violence. This list is a guideline for medical personnel who conduct physical examinations:

- Assess the central distribution area for injury: head, face, neck, ears, throat, thoracic region, abdominal area, buttock, genitals, legs, and arms.
- Examine for bilateral distribution of injuries to multiple areas—lacerations, abrasions, and contusions, bite marks, and evidence of physical trauma.
- Carefully check the mouth and all orifices for tissue damaged by caustic substances.
- Evaluate the period of delay from onset of injury to arrival for medical care—note multiple injuries in their various stages of healing.
- Evaluate the type and extent of injuries in relation to patient's explanation.
- Conduct an extensive evaluation for rape and a pattern of chronic injury.
- Document chronic pain, phychogenic pain, or pain related to diffuse trauma in the absence of conspicuous evidence.
- Evaluate for eating disorders, alcoholism, and drug addiction (illicit and prescription drugs).
- Evaluate pregnant women carefully for domestic violence injuries: Focus on breasts, abdominal and genital areas. Check for substance abuse, malnutrition, depression and anxiety, psychosomatic complaints, and delayed or sporadic use of prenatal care, premature labor, spontaneous abortions, and miscarriages.

- Obtain the patient's permission and photograph visible injuries.

- Document all relevant negative findings, and patient's subjective complaints even though physical evidence is lacking.

The health care provider must always have a professional demeanor, and adhere to all established procedures including maximum levels of competence.

Clinical Charting Format

Clinical charting, which is a vital part of the medical documentation, is essential for treatment as well as legal redress of domestic violence episodes. Medical professionals must become aware that they will be summoned into court to testify in spousal battery and other types of domestic violence cases. Most states are enacting laws to make domestic violence a crime. Even if a victim refuses to press charges, the legal apparatus may pursue prosecution in those cases where the evidence dictates. The interview data gathered during a medical intervention is not only a medical document, but a legal one as well. Thus, the integrity of the medical record must be capable of survival in the court setting. Good clinical practice, medical and psychological, is the hallmark of ending domestic violence because it treats the injuries, educates, and supports arrest and prosecution. The following clinical charting protocol is one standard recommended by the Santa Clara County Domestic Violence Council and Board of Supervisors (1994).

- Provide a detailed description of the patient's injuries preferably on a Domestic Violence Assessment Form, with body charts when applicable. Include age; gender; type, extent, and frequency of injury; location, and patient's explanations.

- Attach photographs of injuries, and other objective evidence such as x-rays, laboratory and tissue analysis reports.

- Obtain a medical and psychosocial history: past treatment for domestic violence, accident proneness, falls, and other injuries. Get the patient's history of alcohol ingestion and drug abuse including that of his or her partner. Record the history of rape, other types of forced sex, and sexually transmitted diseases. Note all behavioral observations of an aggressive, uncooperative, and overly-concerned partner.

- In describing presenting problems, chief complaints, and history of the illness, the medical professional should capture the abusive episodes in the patient's exact words enclosed in quotation marks. Apart from expressed encouragement, the Health Care Provider must not lead the patient nor put words in his or her mouth. Agitation, defensiveness, anger, fear, and anxiety should be noted, and a brief analysis of the discrepancies between the injuries documented and explanations offered by the patient.

- Observational data should include unusual behavior as sanctioned by the patient's culture, so that the medical professional is not using only his or her monocultural value system to evaluate a patient's behavior. Document in detail, scratches, bruises, torn clothes, particularly out-of-season long-sleeve shirts and turtle neck sweaters, and dark glasses. Smeared make-up, broken fingernails, and jewelry are important to document.

- Include in your documentation, the name, precinct number, and telephone number of the investigating police officer. All collateral information from other professionals (psychologists, social workers, clergy), who examined or talked to the patient must be included in your documentation.

- Medical records that document domestic violence are admissible as evidence in a court of law in the United States if: the records were compiled as "a regular course of business," they were gathered in accordance with established organizational procedures, and properly secured with access limited to professional staff only.

Domestic violence is a serious health hazard. It pervades all educational, age, ethnocultural, gender, and socio-economic groups. The medical community, with its expertise to diagnose, document, treat, and provide expert testimony and irrefutable evidence, is a major force in stemming the tide of domestic violence. The following areas are standard procedures medical health providers should carefully attend to in domestic violence cases:

History:
Medical professionals must routinely screen all patients for a past history and active process of domestic violence.

Physical Examination:
When injuries are reported or observed by the health professional, irrespective of how slight, an evaluation for domestic violence including a physical examination must be done.

Interviewing Protocol:
When domestic violence is reported or detected through behavioral and other clinical observation, the health professional should confidentially interview the patient in a private setting. The interviewer's behavior should be non-judgmental, understanding, and supportive. A warm attitude and posture of genuine reaching out can facilitate the patient's comfort level

and willingness to self-disclose. The interviewer should address the patient's safety, and level of lethality including her immediate plans to enter a domestic violence center, return home, or exercise other options.

Assessment of Lethality

We are aware that statistically, a battered woman increases her chances of being severly injured or killed by the batterer when she leaves him. The coordinated efforts of law enforcement, the judiciary, treatment professionals, and other community members are to provide safety services so that the victim increases her chances of not being murdered when she leaves. However, it is critically important for medical professionals to evaluate the lethality or likelihood that a victim can be killed by her batterer. If the doctor or other medical personnel feels incapable or inexperienced in lethality assessments, a psychologist, clinical social worker, or other experienced mental health evaluator should be consulted.

The rationale for a lethality assessment is grounded in victim safety. All spousal batterers are potential murderers; some more than others. Assessment for lethality seeks to determine a batterer's potential to inflict deadly violence on a spouse, ex-spouse, or girlfriend. When the following indicators or factors are present, there is an increased likelihood of homicidal violence. The more factors present, the greater there is a chance or risk of homicide by the batterer.

Spouse as Personal Property

Jealousy and possessiveness are two trade marks of the spousal batterer. A batterer's homicidal rage is often signalled in such statements as, "I'll kill you before I let someone else have you!" "Death before divorce!" "You'll be dead before he gets his hands on you!" These statements epitomize a batterer's basic belief that a spouse or girlfriend is his property, with no right to leave him.

A batterer who threatens his partner, their children, her family members, the household pets, or suicide should be taken seriously, and considered dangerous.

Access to Weapons

If a batterer possesses weapons, has threatened to use them, or has used them previously to perpetrate violence on his spouse or children, his potential to inflict deadly harm is extremely high. The possession of, access to, and use of guns are accurate predictors of homicide. If a batterer has a history of arson, or has threatened arson previously, fire should be viewed as a weapon. Irrespective of his assurances of non-violence, or the victim's corroboration that she will not be harmed, the mental health professional has a responsibility to act immediately when these dynamics are present.

Dependency and Separation Anxiety

Many batterers create and sustain through intimidation and violence a "master-servant" relation with their partner. They develop strong dependency needs in which the partner organizes, and manages from the simple to most complex affairs in their life. Any hints or signs that the victim will leave are rationalized as abandonment and disloyalty punish-able by death. This perceived abandonment, especially if he idolizes her, creates stress, anger, rage, and ideas of retalia-tion. The separation anxiety, and sense of disloyalty may trigger the homicidal rage.

Homicidal Plan

Depression is a prominent feature of the spousal battery problem especially if the batterer is an alcoholic and/or a drug user. Many individuals who suffer from depression are suicidal and homicidal, with the homicidal fantasy aimed at family members. When the batterer has a homicidal plan as to "who," "when," "where," and "how," the greater the likelihood that he will kill someone. The batterer who has rehearsed a suicidal or homicidal fantasy, has a plan, and possesses or has access to a weapon, and views death as a viable option must be placed in the highest risk category. In essence, a more elaborately detailed plan, with greater access to the means, translates into the greatest risk.

Homicidal Signs

Homicide seldom occurs randomly and in isolation from previous violence or other spousal battery dynamics. Intimidation, threats, 911 and other police calls unfold within a context of escalated abuse and other life threatening behaviors. When the batterer loses control, and perpetrates his violent acts seemingly impervious to legal, interpersonal, and societal consequences, lethality is at a dangerously high level. Those restraints that previously contained his homicidal rage may have lost their effectiveness so the spouse's demise is viewed as his last resort.

Targeting the Victim(s)

The batterer, who has access to his spouse, ex-spouse, or girlfriend can perpetrate a homicide with no obstruction. Access to battered women and their children occur through custody visitation and exchange, court appearances, and at a host of other places within the community. If the perpetrator does not have access to the victim he cannot murder her. If his access to their children is supervised by someone besides the spouse, his chances of killing the victim are greatly reduced. Safety services for a victim require the involvement of law enforcement, and the judiciary when the risk of lethality is present.

The Action Phase—When a medical professional determines that a perpetrator is a suicidal risk, and/or a battered woman can be further victimized by his lethal violence, immediate safety sensitive measures must be taken. The victim and law enforcement personnel must be notified immediately, and an ex-parte mental health admission for the batterer initiated as may be appropriate. Whether or not she offers resistance, the battered woman should be apprised of the high lethality danger, and escorted to a Domestic Violence Center with her children (Hart, 1992).

It is not redundant to reemphasize the critical role medical professionals play in treating the battered woman and other victims of domestic violence. However, medical care providers are being called upon to be vigilant and vocal. Their vigilance will increase the identified number of victims treated for domestic violence, and help identify the source of their abuse. Their vocal response will join the voices of many who say domestic violence is illegal, wrong, and deadly.

The Role of Academia

As previously mentioned, domestic violence and spousal battery in particular were America's "dirty secrets," thus colleges and universities did not provide significant training or engaged in the candid discourse accorded other subjects. Academia has a responsibility to develop and teach domestic violence and spousal battery courses. The academic community must demonstrate leadership in this area. Research on causality, program efficacy, and recidivism are some areas for empirical investigation. The professional and lay community alike hunger for accurate, and research-oriented information on the interdisciplinary approach to domestic violence remediation and elimination.

One cannot over emphasize the role of academia in fulfilling its pedagogical function within the espoused mission of public discourse, and to accurately inform its citizenry. Academia has been woefully silent on spousal battery and domestic violence.

Debates, lectures, academic course work, seminars and conferences can ignite the process of public awareness, and preparatory training for domestic violence and spousal battery interventionists. The scourge of domestic violence and spousal battery pervades all educational, socioeconomic, and ethnocultural strata. The invitation for serious scholarly work in family violence has been extended.

Chapter Eight

Counseling the Batterer

Behavioral change is seldom a spontaneous act. It requires a tripartite process of intervention that explores one's emotions, thought processes (belief system, values, attitudes, customs, perceptions), and the dysfunctional behavior itself.

V. Michael McKenzie, Ph.D.

Let us reflect for a moment on the magnitude of this spousal abuse problem as epitomized by the statistics discussed in Chapters One through Three. Juxtapose these alarming and frightening statistics with the beliefs we identified as occurring most frequently among spousal batterers. Then add to the spousal battery equation, all the information you learned in Chapter Four about our socialization processes, and how specifically gender-biased beliefs and behaviors are transmitted to young children in their family context. Factor in the positive reinforcement a spousal batterer or potential batterer receives from his gender-biased parents or caregivers, and extended kin, then add the encouragement he gets from other batterers within his peer group. Imagine the deep rooted gender-biased beliefs of the batterer, and his deeply-entrenched spousal battery behavior. This gives you an authentic picture of the difficulty, complexity, and resistance encountered in attempts to change the dysfunctional behavior of a spousal batterer. Difficulty in changing the spousal batterer's behavior does not signify impossibility.

The Dynamics of Spousal Abuse Change

External Factors—Leverage

One of the expensive lessons learned from the Nicole Brown-Simpson's tragedy pertains to the laissez-faire attitude of those professionals who referred O. J. Simpson to psychotherapy, and the ones who failed to monitor his participation. The professional community, including law enforcement, judiciary, and mental health, was remissed in its responsibility regarding the O. J. Simpson's spousal battery cycle. Arrest, probation, mandatory therapy, consistent monitoring, and incarceration for counseling infractions, and/or the return to spousal battery must be the remedial sequence of activities for rehabilitation. If we are aware that batterers seldom voluntarily seek help because they lack intrinsic motivation, deny they have a problem, minimize the effects of their battering behavior on women and children, and resist cooperating and complying with counseling recommendations, then it behooves us to structure an intervention program that will yield maximum success.

Domestic violence perpetrators are a violent group of offenders, who require the maximum legal and clinical intervention. The explicit goal of this dual legal and clinical intervention is the cessation of violence, safety of the victim, and rehabilitation of batterers. The explicit message is violence against women, children, and family members is intolerable; it will not be condoned under provoked or unprovoked circumstances. Any type of domestic violence, be it intentional or unintentional, is consequential with the onus of responsibility being placed squarely on the perpetrator. As the

San Diego County Task Force on Domestic Violence (1991) aptly emphasized, domestic violence perpetrators must understand that spousal battery, and other forms of violent behavior have serious consequences. These offenders must face arrest, a suspended or deferred sentence, probation, incarceration, counseling, or some combination of these penalties.

It is important to reiterate that if men receive the same or a similar type of socialization, it is reasonable to expect that some degree of gender-biased traits will exist in their behavioral repertoire. Thus, whether we are in law enforcement, the judiciary, mental health, education, the ministry, indeed any profession, our gender-biased value system, irrespective of how subtle, contaminates our professional judgment regardless of how we deny its existence. We may be unreasonably empathic with our male kinship, over-identify with them, or display some other homogeneous trait that compromises our impartiality.

Leverage involves the threat or use of punitive action to force batterers to comply with mandated counseling. Such punitive action may be extended probation, increased fines, and/or incarceration. Leverage may also be a positive reward that awaits a participant when he or she completes counseling, and all other intervention recommendations. The reward may be family reunification if the spouse, children, and other family members receive counseling, and mutually agree on uniting. It could also be the return of driving privileges, which may have been revoked because of a spousal battery incident. Leverage, therefore, is that requisite component of spousal battery intervention that has the distinct probability of positively influencing counseling outcome.

Intervention Process

The Pre-Counseling Agenda

If our goal is to extinguish the scourge of spousal battery, the interdisciplinary treatment approach is our only viable option. The pre-counseling agenda is purposefully designed to enhance therapeutic gains such that the victim, batterer, and community are served in a genuinely effective way.

In this phase, which precedes counseling, the victim is identified, and an assessment of her medical, legal, financial, and other needs made. She is apprised of her legal rights, and assisted in determining and exercising those options deemed appropriate for her current circumstance. Community resources including information about women's domestic violence centers are made available to her. If the victim's injuries are acute, emergency medical services are rendered immediately, followed by the resolution of her other problems. Children must be attended to, with temporary custody being granted to maternal family members, or others identified by the victim as being appropriate. If the battered woman chooses to remain at home, a court order of protection should be issued for her safety. She must be strongly encouraged to enter counseling.

The batterer or offender must be identified, and arrested if sufficient cause exists that he perpetrated a spousal battery crime. This is not the time to be overly-empathic with the batterer because his manipulation, and any expressed compassion may spell doom for the victim. A trained law enforcement officer, who understands the dynamics of domestic violence, would know that arrest is the best he could offer the batterer in the long-run. This is the time when an interventionist must resist his or her biases, and propensity to be anti-victim or pro-batterer. Simultaneously, prosecutory evidence must be collected in a professional manner to aid criminal prosecutions or other legal matters. If the batterer has medical needs these should be attended to professionally, with the appropriate documentation. Regardless of a perceived inability to convict, community standards require placement on probation, mandatory counseling, and strict court or probationary monitoring of the batterer's compliance with intervention goals. Given what we know about the deep-rooted nature of spousal battery, a batterer's denial, violence, minimization, and resistance to rehabilitation, it is preposterous to think that mandated counseling for eight or sixteen hours of anger management can be effective. Meaningful and effective counseling for the batterer can be no less than six months, twenty-six weeks, or fifty-two hours. The ideal should be seventy-five hours spanning a period of six to nine months. Even an astute clinician would require a minimum of six months to move a batterer beyond the superficiality and artificiality of his facade. It requires a six-month period of counseling for a therapist to peel off the layers of defensiveness, and sufficiently engage a perpetrator for an appreciable degree of permanent change.

The treatment team, and its mental health agency must be held to a high standard of accountability. Each referral source must send an information package when the batterer is mandated to counseling. The referral package should contain a legal history including pertinent data about the arrest, and previous battery incidents. Known psychiatric treatment should be referenced or included, and his probation officer's name, telephone number, and business address must be enclosed. Monthly counseling progress reports are to be sent to the client's probation officer, court, and social agency counselor if one is involved in this case. The legal advocate, and guardian *ad litem*, if attached to the court, or women's domestic violence center, must be apprised of the batterer's progress whether or not his wife and children are housed at the center. Any infraction of the intervention contract by the batterer must be reported to his probation officer so that appropriate action can be taken.

The Batterers' Intervention Program

Treating Men Who Batter Women and Children

Spousal battery counseling begins with a comprehensive clinical assessment. This evaluation is necessary to gauge the magnitude of the presenting problem or problems, and provide information for rehabilitation planning. After collecting such identifying data as age, race and marital status, the evaluation focuses on the presenting problem in relation to precipitating events, current symptoms, and the batterer's emotional state. A family and personal history is taken involving the current living situation, family constellation, early growth and development, cultural, religious, peer group, educational, and recreational affiliation. A sexual, substance abuse, legal, and nutritional history is taken. Academic, vocational, and job-related data are gathered. A mental status examination is done to determine suicidal and homicidal ideation, hallucinations, delusions, or other evidence of psychosis. The psychotic individual is generally not able to benefit from spousal battery counseling.

The presence or absence of organic diseases is determined. Present and past medication use is ascertained, and any previous psychiatric treatment discussed. The evaluation process yields valuable information regarding the batterer's level of anger, minimization, and denial, his history of battery, level of insight and motivation, and degree of commitment to the therapeutic process. The batterer's gender-biases and hostility toward his spouse and children are evaluated. His strengths, deficiencies, needs, mood, affect, and previous legal troubles are included in the diagnostic picture. These data are integrated, processed, and used to identify the problem areas a batterer needs to work on. If there is an alcohol or a drug abuse problem, counseling is provided concurrently, but separate and apart from spousal battery intervention. The counseling plan is designed as a concretized cognitive map that guides the problem-solving therapeutic process. During this evaluation, the batterer is apprised of his responsibility including attendance, full self-disclosure, active participation, confidentiality, and practice of his newly acquired skills. All his questions are addressed. Whether or not the spousal battery group facilitator, or some other clinician does the comprehensive assessment, the group leader has an in-depth clinical background on each group participant before he enters the group process. This advantage allows the group leader to validate or invalidate the information self-disclosed by participants, or nudge them along when fear, anxiety, or manipulation impede their emotional honesty. Most importantly, this evaluation determines if a batterer is appropriate for and can benefit from the intervention protocol.

Pre-group

Batterers and victims are not to be treated in the same group. On rare occasions a spouse or girlfriend may make a guest appearance to satisfy an urge to experience the group process. She may be curious about what the batterer reports regarding his motivation, level of group participation, or progress, and may want to see him in action, talk to the leader, or other group members. Written permission from group members to videotape sessions is a viable answer to this request.

Written interorganizational agreements should be undertaken between the treating facility, and domestic violence centers, courts, probation officers, legal advocates, and guardians *ad litem* to allow monitoring. This is critical especially if the victim is in a women's domestic violence center, or elsewhere, and has a desire for re-unification. The monitoring person, who sits in the group periodically, may be able to offer a different and objective view on the batterer's readiness for reunification. This is not quite in vogue, so the professional community may be resistant. Court mandated participants, who have violated the Domestic Violence Law, and whose battering behavior includes its inherent secrecy, will find that their behavioral change requires openness to scrutiny by others. Monitoring personnel will sign all necessary confidentiality releases so that only those with "the need to know" will be apprised. This procedure has worked in Dade City, Florida to the satisfaction of victim, batterer, and professional.

The First Group

Spousal battery intervention groups should only be same gender or homogeneous in their composition. It is critical in the rehabilitation process to incorporate the woman's perspective so that men gain directly some insight of how their behavior impacts on the female psyche. Many female perpetrators have also been victims; their input through videotapes is valuable especially when empathic skills are taught in the group. Additionally, a female group co-facilitator is a vital member of the rehabilitation process; she elicits gender-biased and other transferential reactions that allow for growth-oriented processing. Some other advantages of an inter-gender co-facilitating team would include:

- Shared responsibility that alternates between presenting content and managing group process

- The modeling of intergender communication, respect, conflict resolution strategies, and gender equity; modeling professional competence from the female perspective is therapeutically valuable

- Co-facilitators provide a source of support for each other, give and receive feedback, and forestall burnout, which is prevalent in mental health counseling

One of the most significant occurrences in the Spousal Battery Counseling Group is the self-introduction required of each new member, and the telling of his story as we have labeled it. Group members have learned from their previous self-introduction and confrontation how to observe, how to listen, what to listen for, and how to confront the new member. The group participants listen to the new self-introductions with a caring seriousness that says spousal battery is not a joking matter, and we are here to help. The group listens for the feelings and emotional states (anger, rage, fear, jealousy, frustration, hostility, envy). They listen for denial of the problem, and an inability to take responsibility or ownership for the battering behavior. They listen for blaming ("She hit me first," "My wife provoked the attack," "I was drunk, and she still kept messing with me," "I hit her to stop the nagging"), and the minimization ("I just pushed her," "I only slapped her once," "I hit her with an open hand," "It's no big deal—we worked it out," "I just pulled her hair," "I didn't mean to hurt her"). They listen keenly for the gender-biased beliefs epitomized in the overt or covert put-down of women, the sexist humor, and vulgar insults. They attend to the non-verbal language (gestures and facial expressions), and pay strict attention to patronizing remarks about women, and children including expressed anger and other types of hostility. They help the batterer to recognize the incongruency between what he says he feels and how he behaves (the professed love for his spouse and simultaneous physical-emotional abuse). They confront firmly and supportively.

The group examines the batterer's psychological defense structure, and his need to dominate, control, and inflate his ego through the vicious attacks, innuendos, assaults, and physical abuse he directs at his partner. Quite often, two or three group members will attempt to rescue the new participant because they cannot stomach the pain and anxiety the newcomer experiences, which is reminiscent of what they felt on their first day of confrontation. Sometimes the rescuing is associated with the male kinship (complicity and collusion) of taking care of a fellow batterer. Irrespective of its source or origin, the rescuers are, and must be confronted by the group. The group calls them on their counterproductive behavior, and re-teaches them a more healthy way of dealing with their feelings. In such rescuing attempts, group members would point out that if the rescuers were practicing emotional honesty and focusing on their own recovery, they would have honestly self-disclosed to the group what thoughts and feelings were evoked in them when the new participant was confronted. This would have allowed them to reach deep within to wrestle with their thoughts and feelings instead of externalizing their focus on another person's emotional state, thus avoiding their internal state of discomfort. Disclosure to and feedback from the group further consolidate their internal centering, thus enhancing their skill development, and that of other group members.

This is the approach or technique that begins the change process immediately for a new group participant, while it gives old group members additional opportunity to recognize defensiveness, emotional dishonesty, incongruency in thinking, feeling, and behaving. They are then able to practice confrontation, and other behavioral interventions on themselves and others. The explicit message and theme are respect for women and children on all levels, and cessation of physical violence and verbal abuse.

The philosophy of this treatment approach with batterers incorporates principles from: Rational Emotive Therapy, Rational Behavior Therapy, Client Centered Therapy, Substance Abuse Treatment Models, the Duluth Domestic Abuse Intervention Project, the San Diego County Standards for the treatment of domestic violence perpetrators, and the Tripartite Spousal Battery Intervention Model developed by this author. The psychoeducational intervention in this counseling milieu postulates that our patriarchal society inculcates gender-biased values, and gives the male an indelible belief system that he is superior, entitled, and privileged. This value system of entitlement and privilege is self-empowering to such an extent that the male batterer invokes his special status to intimidate; coerce; threaten; abuse economically, emotionally, and physically; minimize; deny; and blame his victim or victims for the violent behavior he uses to dominate and control them. His internal philosophy and manifested behavior center on the crooked misperception and dysfunctional belief that he has the right to use force against women.

This propensity to batter, which is grounded in the gender-biased belief system is perpetuated by peer group influences either through silent collusion or complicity, or the boastful fellowship of batterers. What forms the profile of a batterer's mentality and behavior is a personality core that symbolizes the maltreatment of women and children.

The thoughts, emotions, and violent behavior are the lethal foundation of spousal battery. This TEB diagram depicts some of these thoughts, emotions, and behavioral patterns of spousal batterers.

Thoughts, Emotions, and Behavior (TEB) Patterns

Thought Processes	Emotions	Behavior Emotional & Physical
Cognitive Content/Beliefs	Feeling States	Expressions
To have rights over her life To foster dependency To be in control To isolate her from family and friends To demonstrate he is in charge His needs come first She should cater to me The man is king of his castle I control the household and finances Women are for men's pleasure She deserves abuse I have the right to be in control Women cannot be trusted She is dumb and fat The bitch is lazy I am privileged I am in charge She is an object She is inferior The weaker sex Sex object Servant	Anger Fear Jealousy Hate Self-hate Self-pity Insecure Envious Vengeful Neglectful Frustrated Unappreciated Resentment Feeling stressed Worthless Threatened Suspicious Defensive Hostile Enraged Agitated Shame Poor self-concept Depressed	Interrogates spouse and sexually harasses her (whore, slut, bitch) Insults and humiliates her Monitors her activities Sarcastic and condescending Calls friends to check up on her Stops her from leaving Demands she cooks and cleans Rummages through her purse Embarrasses her in front of family, friends, and strangers Pulling her hair Rubbing food in her hair Making her beg for food or other necessities Calling her names (dumb, ugly, fat) Accuse her of infidelity Discloses his unfaithfulness Physical violence Invading her space Sexual abuse

After the batterer tells his "story" in the first session, he is then required to internally center on what it means to be a batterer. He must inwardly and outwardly accept that he is a batterer as the first step in breaking his denial, minimization, and blaming. He must take responsibility, and be accountable for his behavior by acknowledging first he is a batterer, then making a commitment to work through his violent temperament, and gender-biased beliefs. He later processes empathically what his partner experienced before, during, and after his emotional abuse and physical violence.

The Tripartite Process of Spousal Battery

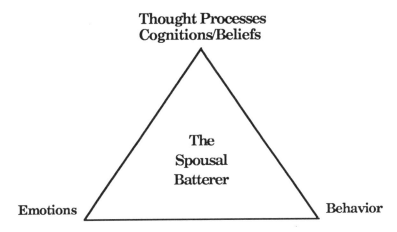

The Interplay of thoughts, feelings, and behavior in Spousal Battery

The predominant feeling and thinking among batterers are that their anger, substance abuse, alcoholism, stress, and/or abusive-violent upbringing cause their spousal battery, and other types of family violence. It is unacceptable in domestic violence counseling to accept excuses and the assignment of blame. A batterer must be accountable and take responsibility for his violent behavior unconditionally. The Tripartite Process of Domestic Violence is designed to disarm the batterer from his crutch of excuses, and assist him through awareness to take full responsibility for his actions.

Behavior and Emotions: It is quite easy to identify the batterer's behavior because it is always documented in court papers. Additionally, the admission or intake assessment documents other behaviors that are placed on the list, with which the perpetrator is confronted. Once we establish that these are the behaviors of the batterer, we zoom in by asking, what caused these behaviors? The reasons, excuses, explanations, rationale, and justification flow profusely. "I was upset, angry, and drunk." "She pushed me too far." "She hit me first." "I did not mean to hurt her." The group re-focuses on the question, who caused this behavior? After some circular defensiveness, most blame the victim, some regress into "I don't know," while a few take responsibility partially.

The confrontation begins with a focus on the batterer's "crooked" and "irrational" thinking that someone else caused his violent behavior. We point out that only if the battered woman or victim has magical powers can she cause him to batter her. We also point out that no one who has magical powers would use it so self-destructively. As the batterer begins to sense what we are saying, we intensify our focus. No one can make you batter. It is a choice the batterer exercises of his own free will. No one has the power to make you or any other man batter a woman. We hammer the point that battery is a choice. The question why the abuser batters has not been answered substantively. So we re-focus, and continue the confrontation.

When a man batters in response to his anger, jealousy, fear, frustration, perceived provocation, other emotions, or emotional states, he is engaging in an automatic response devoid of thinking or other types of cognitive processing. According to the Tripartite Process of Spousal Battery, the batterer has an emotional and behavioral reaction without thinking, which spontaneously sets him on an automatic violence response (AVR) mode. This automatic violence response mode, because it lacks thinking and processing, and emanates from a purely emotional base, qualifies as a habit. A habit according to the *Webster's Dictionary* (1987), is "a behavior pattern acquired by frequent repetition, a settled tendency or usual manner of behavior," "an acquired mode of behavior that has become nearly or completely involuntary," "mental-makeup," "implies a doing unconsciously and often impulsively." If we accept the logic that the offender has an emotional-behavioral battery pattern, and we understand that the emotional-behavioral mode is a habit, then it becomes easy to see that a habit is akin to compulsively irresponsible behavior. If battery can be equated with a habit, then this compulsive behavior presents a formidable task to change agents. We do not excuse the violent or irresponsible behavior of alcoholics, or those addicted to drugs as in the vigorous prosecution of drunk drivers. Similarly, the behavior of batterers should not be excused.

Offenders gain insight into the emotional connection to their battering behavior. They begin to understand that the habit or emotional-behavioral mode will always result in a violent spousal encounter. When we make demands that a woman behave according to our wishes, and she does not, we are left with anger. To enforce our demand, we resort to physical force. This is the behavioral pattern of a batterer. The goal is to help the offender see, understand, and stop the automatic battering behavior in response to his emotions that may spring from unmet demands to control and dominate women. He learns to get in touch with his emotions, center on them instead of acting them out. In the case of anger, he is taught to recognize its signs and symptoms, and how to diffuse it instead of acting it out in a counterproductive way. In essence, the batterer learns to put some distance between his emotions and the behavioral responses he has allowed them to precipitate. What emerges is a constellation of techniques or skills for emotional recognition, and the management of those dysfunctional behaviors he previously used in response to his feelings. Besides recognizing the signs of his anger, he resists the impulse to use the old behaviors. He learns to confront the source of his anger appropriately, to share his feelings in a non-accusatory and non-judgmental manner, and to self-disclose in a respectful instead of hostile manner. He asks instead of demands what he wants or needs, and is respectfully tolerable of a negative response or rejection. As he practices with feedback and encouragement, the batterer becomes comfortable with facing the source of his emotions and working through his feelings with the person or persons involved. He uses his newly acquired communication, anger management, and interpersonal skills. As he applies these skills, his self-confidence increases. His resocialization has begun, but it has a long course ahead.

Thought Processes — Belief System: Recall that the question regarding where a batterer's behavior originates was not answered. We now answered the rhetorical question. The spouse is not responsible for a batterer's behavior because she does not possess any magical powers to make him act violently or otherwise. We teach that the batterer's violent behavior originates in his thought processes or belief system. The batterer's irrational belief system, which houses his values, biases, ethnic, cultural, and other assumptions, gender role and other stereotypes, colors his perceptions, evaluations, and interpretations of a woman's behavior. His attitude toward women is based on this belief system, and the internal dialogue he engages in, consciously and unconsciously, when interacting with women. If he believes, for instance, that women are inferior, incapable, unequal to men, sex objects, his property, instruments of pleasure, less intelligent, less competent, emotionally fragile, dependent, hysterical malcontents, and deserving of their subordinated status, he is more than likely to treat them with contempt, disrespect, disdain, cruelty, abuse, and humiliation. When we add the eleven gender-biased beliefs, and their variations found most commonly among batterers, as depicted in Chapter Three, we have a sense of the deeply embedded bias that forms the male attitude toward women.

Change in behavior and attitude toward women involves a re-socialization process in which the batterer is helped in his transition from dominance, power, and control over women to one of intergender equity. To achieve intergender balance or equity, the batterer must again look inward at his values, attitudes, and their behavioral manifestations. In domestic violence counseling, the immediate and short-term goal is a cessation of the violence against women and children. Many abusers believe their violent behavior is a solution to a spouse or girlfriend's provocation, and their emotionally unthinking physical reaction is justified. In the Batterers' Intervention Program, we condemn violence in language, attitude, thinking, and behaving. We foster non-violent thinking and behaving. We offer non-violent options for solving conflicts or disputes. We explore violence as a tactic of dominance and control; then the concept of non-violence is processed.

We define non-violent behavior on the emotional or feeling, cognitive or thinking, behavioral or acting levels. Non-violent behavior is the cessation of violent acts against persons and property as a permanent lifestyle change in principle, philosophy, and behavior. It involves an emotional detachment from the symbols, posture, and use of physical force. It uses cognitive restructuring of perceptions, thoughts, and beliefs to change threats and acts of violence, and demonstrate they are not viable options for establishing and achieving personal goals. When we modify or extinguish the thoughts and beliefs, and emotional attachment to violent behavior toward women and children, we automatically replace them with a healthy and adaptive set of skills. First, we reiterate that the goal of domination, control and power over women is unhealthy and dysfunctional; it places the batterer on a path of violence. So we change the personal goal of domination, control, and power to one that allows the batterer to express his needs without threat and violence. In a reciprocal manner, the batterer understands and learns that a spouse or partner has an equal right to express herself in a safe and secure environment.

As this non-threatening and non-violent philosophy begins to take hold, the batterer learns how to end his intimidation tactics. He has already developed skills to identify the signs and symptoms of anger, fear, jealousy, frustration, and other feelings and emotional states. He knows how to confront the source of his feelings with respect, and self-disclose his internal reactions (feelings and thoughts). Now he focuses on respectful interpersonal communication. Emotional honesty with his spouse regarding his feelings and behavior, building trust and giving unconditional support, working on a partnership of bona fide equality, mastering negotiation and conflict resolution skills become the central focus. Adult responsibility and accountability during marital conflicts, arguments, or fights are explored regarding a possible return of the old dysfunctional behaviors.

Male sexual conduct in relationships plagued by spousal battery is considered carefully and seriously. Batterers are taught to take seriously, and respect a woman's right to say no to his sexual advances and exploits. The marriage contract is not a passport for sexual access when a woman resists conjugal advances. Sexual intercourse in healthy marriages and other unions is a mutual expression of intimacy. In the context of spousal battery, sexual relations become unpleasant, crude, one-sided, objectionable, and uncomfortable. Women often report that they are bullied and violated.

Forcible sex, sexual abuse, sexual assault, and other types of sexual rape wreak painful havoc on the psychic of many wives and girlfriends. Women are repulsed by the thought of having sex with the batterer, and freeze emotionally and physically when touched. A woman's inability to protect her private parts, and prevent a batterer from violating her person, makes her vulnerable, with a sense of shame and shattered self-image. The batterer is allowed through the psychoeducational process to gain insight and develop empathy for the victim he sexually molests. We focus on the manifestation of sexual violence through the following behaviors:

- Sexual battery and marital rape.
- Forcible sex when a spouse is asleep.
- Calling her names such as frigid and barren.
- Forcing her into deviant sex acts.
- Inserting objects into her vagina and rectum.
- Infecting her with sexually transmitted diseases.
- Blaming her for low or no sexual gratification.
- Rough and painful sex designed to hurt a woman.
- Examining and smelling her underwear.
- Discussing her sexual behavior with others.
- Forcing her into pornographic activity.
- Humiliating her and forcing her to beg for intimacy.
- Using sex as a punishment or reward.
- Demanding she have sex with other men, women, or couples.
- Withholding affection and intimacy.
- Flirting in her presence.
- Accusing her of infidelity.

- Smearing her face and body with semen, urine, or other secretions.
- Forcing her to dress as a prostitute in private and public.

The goal is to list as many variations of sexual violence as the group is capable of generating. Group members must be encouraged and persuaded to self-disclose their coercive and violent sexual acts perpetrated on their victims. Women who have been sexually victimized by batterers, and other offenders must be supported in revealing this pain and anger in the recovery processes. Participants are facilitated to struggle openly with their feelings and experiences for individual, and the collective growth. The cathartic release is designed to discharge the pent up hostility and deep-seated pain. Empathy, or the ability to understand what a woman feels, or how she feels when sexually dominated and violated is the goal of this section. Individuals close their eyes and listen, and visualize the hurt they have inflicted on their victims. They are asked to share their internal commitment to a non-violent lifestyle. They are encouraged to give feedback to the group on their feelings and thoughts, and sense of what the victim feels when she is sexually molested or violated. We generate a victims' list.

Sexual Victimization Effects on a Spouse

Cheap	Hurt	Unclean
Abused	Alone	Victimized
Dirty	Debased	Anger
Assaulted	Raped	Humiliated
Inadequate	Inferior	Depersonalized
Dehumanized	Low	Discarded
Shabby	Vile	Degraded
Distrustful	Cold	Distant

Before the group moves to set goals for achieving sexual respect, individuals express what insights they have gotten from the group processing. When this is accomplished, three volunteers summarize what the group processed and discussed.

Acquiring Attitudes of Sexual Respect

Sexual respect becomes a deeply ingrained attitude that is not easily swayed or influenced by past disrespect for women, or any anti-female philosophy or sentiments. Sexual respect is conveyed in those male behaviors that communicate positive regard for a woman's sexuality, her right to say no without having to defend it, and a man's acceptance of her positive or negative sexual expression. Sexual respect is an attitude that values and esteems rather than condemns or ridicules a woman's intimate choices. Sexual respect is the dignity and nobility inherent in a man's acceptance of a woman's need to be affectionate, but non-sexual if she chooses to. Sexual respect is a woman's freedom to touch her partner without the obligation to go further. Sexual respect involves heeding the warning when a woman says "Stop!" It means to desist from sexualizing an encounter when she says "no."

The Variations of Sexual Respect:

- Sexual respect does not mean a man has the right to intercourse because he is married to his partner and provides economically for her.
- Sexual respect does not mean if a woman says no she is manipulating, using sex conditionally, or having an affair.
- Sexual respect does not mean a woman should dutifully surrender sexually if she does not have the urge.

- Sexual respect does not mean a man can forcefully indulge in intercourse or rape his partner.

- Sexual respect does not mean a man can manipulate his partner into sexual intercourse by threatening divorce, economic reprisal, or infidelity.

- Sexual respect does not mean if she politely refuses that this would be held against her, and result in his sexual withholding.

- Sexual respect does not mean an angry response, and return to his old dysfunctional behaviors because she said no.

- Sexual respect involves trust in your partner's emotional honesty that her refusal is not an arbitrary, or deliberate rejection to hurt you, and cause you discomfort, but is predicated on a need, desire, or want that requires your mature support.

- Sexual respect has an empathic quality that allows the male partner to draw closer instead of being distant at a time when his spouse may be experiencing some difficulty in her life.

- Sexual respect is the mutuality inherent in a healthy and equal partnership that relishes tenderness, intimacy, increased communication, and non-sexual sharing when a spouse has reason to say "no" or "not now" to her partner.

- Sexual respect is a building block for the spontaneous glow or sparkle that ignites a couple's libido, and propels them to that delightful plateau of marital bliss.

- Sexual respect is the inner sense of dignity and security a man possesses that allows him to be supportive, non-punitive and loving, without feeling rejected, when his partner says "no."

The rehabilitation of these spousal batterers is now in the re-socialization phase, where new concepts and skills are taught, practiced, and mastered. Meaningful and effective communication within the context of a marriage or other intimate relationship is stressed. Interpersonal feedback is the giving and receiving of information about how one's behavior is affecting others, and what impact the behavior of others is having on the recipient. For example, if your spouse or girlfriend refuses for the second or third time to have sexual intercourse with you, and you become angry, depressed, with resentment and a sense of rejection, what do you do? Return to the old abusive behaviors is not the correct response, it is strongly discouraged. The following scenario is an example of what is taught and processed:

Awareness of Feelings

The batterer must first get in touch with what he is feeling. The impulse to act immediately interferes with the process of recognizing his feelings, and may even propel him to behave inappropriately. So he focuses on the symptoms of his anger, and other feelings, which, although general for most human beings, are unique to him. These may include accelerated heart beat, and increased pulse rate, blood pressure, and other cardiovascular functions. Tension, anxiety, and a general physiological tightness may be experienced. Blurred vision, neck pain, stomach tightness, stuttering, quietness, and poor eye contact may be symptomatic of his anger. Passive aggressive behaviors, such as kicking walls or doors, slamming objects, increasing the volume on a television or radio, or mumbling, are counterproductive ways of releasing his hostility. There are other signs and symptoms of anger that are unique to the individual he or she may already be aware of. To act without recognizing his feelings

can be disastrous because he is allowing himself to unknowingly be controlled by his emotions. He has to admit to himself
what he is feeling and why.

The batterer must then check his thought processes to
gauge what thoughts or beliefs may be feeding his anger. If
his internal dialogue, self-talk, or irrational belief system
says to him, "she is doing it to me again," "the bitch is cheating on me," "she is punishing me with sex again," "I hate her
manipulation," "I am going to fix her ass," and "see, she is
not trying to get along," he is likely to become more angry. If
however, the batterer draws on his group learning skills, and
tunes into his rational belief system, he is likely to think in the
following way: "I have committed to being respectful of my
wife's decisions about her body, although I do not like being
rejected in this way, I will not treat it as awful or catas-
trophic. Empathy means I will try to understand what she is
feeling, or where she is coming from: I will be less centered
on my needs, and do what our partnership requires. I will
find out how she feels, and share with her what I am feeling."
This may seem noble, or artificial, even strange. It generally
is unfamiliar to the person who is not used to processing his
or her emotions, thoughts, and behavior. It takes a short
period of practice for one to become familiar with, and proficient in processing emotions, gauging thought processes to
understand them, and managing their effects on one's behavior. In the period of unfamiliarity with this process, the
participant may require some fifteen or twenty minutes to
complete the self-evaluation process. Frustration, resistance,
and a feeling of wanting to abandon the process may ensue.
We encourage participants to stay with the process because as
they complete one cycle, they move closer to becoming more
functional.

Once the batterer, or anyone else, has completed this
internal analysis (emotions and thoughts), he is ready to

engage in the appropriate behavior. This analysis heightens his awareness so he has a choice regarding how he wishes to behave. The scenario involving the batterer and his wife is used herein to illustrate effective intra and interpersonal communication. In the spirit of equal partnership, more effective communication, and respect for his spouse's sexuality, the batterer's next move is to have a talk with his partner to share his feelings rather than cover them up and act them out inappropriately. He is, in essence, giving her feedback on his reaction to her behavior, or the impact of her behavior on him. The giving and receiving of feedback has rules, and by now the batterer would have mastered the art of interpersonal feedback. This is a brief review of the rules governing feedback.

- Feedback is descriptive rather than judgmental or evaluative. It is constructive and appropriate to focus on what your partner said and did rather than evaluate or interpret her behavior with statements of what you think she is.

- Feedback is specific rather than general or global. It focuses on the feelings originating within the batterer, who has experienced his partner's request, and other behavior.

- Feedback has a time element attached to it. It is most helpful when offered immediately after the behavior has occurred, and it is fresh in the participant's mind.

- Feedback is given about behavior that the recipient can change. Frustration may arise when a person is offered feedback on some defect he or she has no control over.

- Feedback should never be imposed. After feedback is offered, it is left to the recipient to use it how he or she sees fit.

- Feedback is for the benefit of the recipient. It should never be designed for the "dumping" or "unloading" of one's emotional baggage.

- For effective communication, the recipient of feedback should be asked what she or he heard and understood the batterer or whomever to have said. If the paraphrase is essentially what was intended, the giver of feedback should voice his or her satisfaction. If major elements of the feedback were missed, appropriate corrections are permissible.

The batterer whose partner refused to have sex with him would give her feedback in this manner using the skills he has learned.

Batterer: "Marsha (or honey) I would like to talk with you about our present sexual relations. What I would like to say should not take any longer than a few minutes. When can we talk?"

The batterer is calm, non-accusatory, and shows consideration for her by not demanding, or unilaterally deciding she must talk now, or on his terms. If she resents his previous marathon lectures, this commitment to a shorter time of a few minutes would be a respectful consideration. He is on the right track thus far.

The batterer's spouse or partner can respond in one of four ways. "I really don't want to hear what you have to say." "I don't have the time right now." "Maybe—I don't really know." "I would like that very much, how about after dinner tonight." Most of these answers can trigger a hostile response in the batterer, even if he has done well in counseling. Batterers whether they are in or have completed counseling risk relapse. Provocation, intentional or unintentional, his accurate perception or misperception, are no excuse for a rehabilitated batterer to return to his dysfunctional behavior. Secondly, respect for his partner's decision is his motto and guiding principle. If she refuses to talk with him, he can ask her to reconsider because he believes what he has to say is important to their communication and partnership. He can even solicit assistance from their mutual support system to help facilitate this meeting only after she agrees, or is aware of his desire to seek outside help. Since we are teaching feedback skills let us assume she has agreed to talk.

Batterer: "Marsha I appreciate (or thanks for) the time you set aside for us to talk. This means a lot to me (pause). Remember yesterday when you said you preferred if we didn't have sex for a while (he waits for an affirmative response), well, I felt upset, and thought that was unfair to me or even us.

"I am trying to be fair, but I felt you made a decision that affects both of us all by yourself, and left me no choice but to comply. I felt hurt and rejected, and that my feelings weren't important to you.

"I might have been less disturbed by this, but it's the third time in four weeks you have made this request. I must admit that it has crossed my mind that you might have something going on at work. That's all I have to say."

How would you rate his behavior thus far? Has the batterer observed all the rules, or at least the relevant ones pertaining to giving interpersonal feedback? Has there been evaluative, judgmental, or attacking behavior? Has he unloaded on her emotionally or in a hostile way? Was he accusatory? Has he demonstrated sexual respect and inter-gender sensitivity?

The batterer did exceedingly well in offering feedback to his partner. He succeeded in putting the issue into perspective by stating what his concern was, when it originated, how many times, and how he felt about it. He was vague and non-specific when he said, ". . . It has crossed my mind if you have something going on at work." He was alluding to an affair, which required more specificity. We applaud his honest self-disclosure. Additionally, he did not ask his partner, the recipient of the feedback, what she heard him to have said. So the opportunity for her to repeat what she heard and attended to was lost. In giving feedback it is not appropriate to ask "why." The "why" question is not only parental, it borders on amateur psychologizing. "Why" questions take feedback from the realm of how a partner's behavior has impacted on the batterer to more digging into the partner's motivation, needs, and impulses. "Why" deals with cause and not the effect, the latter being the essence of giving feedback. "Why" questions change the focus of the feedback. It is more for the satisfaction of the giver of feedback rather than the recipient.

It is permissible to ask the recipient of feedback to react or respond. If she refuses to give her reactions, her behavior must be respected, and not used manipulatively to say she is guilty of hiding something. The only responsibility of the batterer in giving feedback is to state his feelings and thoughts in a caring, non-evaluative, and non-judgmental way. If the partner or recipient of his feedback chooses to spontaneously self-disclose, answer the unstated "why" question, or empathize with his feelings, then the couple has benefited maximally from the process. If he demands that she behave according to his wishes, wants, or desires, he has violated the tenets of effective interpersonal feedback. When feedback is given in a non-judgmental, non-evaluative, and non-accusatory manner, without demands on the recipient, she is likely to feel psychologically and physically safe. This allows her to listen more non-defensively. If the giver of feedback follows the rules appropriately, and the recipient becomes defensive then the responsibility for the failed outcome is on her.

The Final Intervention Phase

When a spousal batterer understands the role of his gender-biased beliefs in his violent behavior, engages in a resocialization process, and masters self-analysis and communication skills, his prognosis for equitable intergender relations is excellent. The batterer's intervention group continues to reinforce his motivation by helping him to see the positive rewards in gender equity. The anger, hostility, manipulation, emotional dishonesty, sexual disrespect, distrust, emotional and physical abuse, threats, violence, unfairness, dominance, control, exercise of power, verbal abuse, and a multitude of other counterproductive behaviors subside appreciably as the batterer continues the rehabilitation process. The skill-building, and hands-on tools acquisition continue unabated.

The Behavioral Change Plan (BCP)

The behavioral change plan targets specific behaviors the batterer identifies unilaterally or with assistance from counselors, group participants, or his support system.

This behavioral change plan identifies three goals a batterer can work on in his pursuit of equity and a non-violent partnership with his spouse or girlfriend. He may choose to identify other goals of interest to him and his partner. Some common goals may include: shared household responsibilities, greater emotional honesty, building self-esteem and trust, showing respect publicly and privately, support for her educational and career goals, healthy intimacy and sexual relations, and greater accountability and responsibility for his behavior. The themes in spousal battery counseling, including the behavioral change plan, are non-violence, respect, and equity. Meaningful and lasting change is intertwined in these three themes.

The Behavioral Change Plan (BCP)

Name: **Date:**

	Specific Behavioral Actions	Frequency	Duration
Goal 1	To assume more direct parental responsibility at home		
A	Feed both of our children	Once a day	Ninety days
B	Put children to bed	3 times weekly	Ninety days
C	Wash and dry dishes	3 times weekly	Sixty days
Goal 2	Give up dominant and controlling behaviors		
A	Make financial decisions together	As required	Six months
B	Each adult gets equal monetary allowance	Bi-weekly	Six months
C	Stop quizzing and checking up on her	Daily	Six months
D	Don't judge spouse and her friends	Daily	Six months
E	Examine self-talk related to dominance and control of partner	Daily	Six months
F	Stop examining spouse's underwear and rummaging through her pocketbook	Daily	Six months
Goal 3	Stop threats and physical violence with spouse immediately		
A	Identify and relinquish all intimidation expressed in verbal and non-verbal behavior	Daily	Six months
B	Stop throwing objects and invading partner's personal space	Daily	Six months
C	Desist from physical force and all violent behavior	Daily	Permanent
	Behavioral change plan review __ 1 Month __ 3 Months __ Other Identify progress, obstacles, and goal modifications: Add recommitments		
	Signature(s)		

Any spousal batterer who wants to change can do so if he is serious about change, and applies himself diligently in the spousal battery intervention process. Change is difficult and painful, but not impossible. The technology for change is in place, and it is consistently being refined. Domestic violence is learned behavior; spousal battery is a choice offenders make. Domestic violence can be unlearned, and spousal battery can be expunged from one's behavioral repertoire. The days are rapidly ending where a batterer could commit a violent domestic act or spousal battery with impunity. Domestic violence and spousal battery are consequential acts that will be punished to the fullest extent of the law. Get help now—immediately—and break this intergenerational cycle of violence against women, children, siblings, and the elderly.

Chapter Nine

From Victim to Survivor

If there are no ducks, hunters would go home empty-handed. Similarly, if there are no victims, there would not be any spousal battery perpetrators.

V. Michael McKenzie, Ph.D.

Any woman who is in a relationship plagued by domestic violence or spousal battery, whether her involvement be voluntary or involuntary, is a victim. Spousal battery victimization means emotional, psychological, and physical harm and suffering inflicted by a batterer and endured by a victim. Promise of change from the perpetrator, hopes of change generated within the victim, matrimonial vows and religious values, excuses of financial dependence, claims of tolerating abuse for the children's sake, fear, anxiety, and procrastination, when they foster complacency and solidify intransigence, clearly constitute victimization. Victimization is the emotional, cognitive, and behavioral responses to a perpetrator's dominance, control, and exercise of power over a woman. Physical removal, or the spontaneous departure from a spousal battery setting does not change one's status from victim to survivor. The geographical change of residence, which is a commendable first step, does not address the emotional, psychological, physical, and behavioral manifestations of domestic violence or spousal battery, which authentically constitute victimization.

It is only when a victim enters counseling or some other healing process does she begin to break the intergenerational cycle of victimization. Until a victim is able to resolve her psychic pain, deal with dependency, passivity, battered women's syndrome, shattered self-esteem, depersonalization, emotional numbness, and other psychological impairment, she remains a victim. As a victim, she is likely to re-enter the previously violent relationship, or choose a new batterer. When the victim engages in therapy, the process must first be supportive in restoring an appreciable level of inner security to enable her to move forward. The therapeutic process seeks to energize the victim toward a new or renewed sense of purpose, growth, and the development of alternative behaviors that will achieve her desired goals (Blocher, 1974).

A survivor is one who therapeutically faces and resolves her psychological problems pre-dating and resulting from the emotional abuse and physical violence sustained in a spousal battery relationship. The survivor, whose endurance, fortitude, tolerance, and stamina are testimony to her coping skills and survivability rather than character deficits, must be given non-judgmental support, unconditional understanding, and empathic acceptance in the therapeutic process. Those who have not experienced spousal battery particularly in a sustained manner cannot honestly claim to understand the magnitude of a victim's suffering. As counselors, social workers, psychiatric nurses, psychiatrists, and psychologists, we must hold our negative evaluations, and judgmental tendencies in abeyance if we intend or expect to be effective help-ing the battered woman. Therapists can victimize the battered woman a second time, and more severely with their lack of professionalism. Stereotyping, amateurish interventions, negative beliefs and criticisms, snobbish and condescending attitudes can further damage a survivor's psyche. An unhealthy counselor, who has not resolved her own victimization or other psychological baggage, and the male therapist who may have battered, or who subscribes to a gender-biased philosophy cannot be helpful to the battered woman until he or she has worked through his or her own issues.

A number of psychologists (McKenzie, 1985; Pedersen, Lonner and Draguns, 1976; San Diego County Task Force on Domestic Violence, 1991; Rogers, 1961; Sue, 1981) have identified a list of characteristics an effective counselor must have. This writer has modified these to be applicable to spousal battery counseling.

- Effective counselors are able to free themselves from their cultural encapsulation to genuinely share a battered woman's psychic pain, perspective on life, anger, grief, and other psychological reactions likely to be labelled as maladaptive.

- They are aware of their own values, biases, and assumptions about human beings and their behavior, and understand that those of the culturally different person, and battered women in general are different.

- They are aware that environment and culture shape behavior, and that adaptive responses in one context can easily be misunderstood and incorrectly labeled as deviant or sick in another setting.

- The effective counselor is skilled in reaching out to the battered woman, promoting trust, inspiring self-confidence, and demonstrating caring and respect.

- Effective counselors seek to understand rather than judge or condemn. They do not abuse or use the battered woman to fulfill their own needs.

- Effective counselors have specific knowledge and expertise in domestic violence that are of special value in helping battered women.

- Counselors who work with battered women, and other domestic violence survivors—must themselves be violence-free in their own lives, not use illicit drugs or abuse alcohol, be free of gender-biased attitudes and behavior, and not have criminal convictions for immoral acts.

The successful outcome of counseling or psychotherapy is largely dependent on a counselor or therapist's training, experience, skill, and good will. Domestic violence survivors must be educated consumers, and check the educational and experiential background of the therapists from whom they seek assistance. Family physicians, professional associations such as the American Psychological Association (APA), or the National Association for Social Workers (NASW) can be helpful in recommending a competent counselor.

The Healing Process

When working with the battered woman survivor, counselors must not hesitate in believing her accounts of spousal battery irrespective of how bizarre; they are generally true. Counselors must also validate the expressed and exhibited emotional state and feelings such as her anger, fear, hurt or pain, disgust, regret, and rage. If you are a battered woman, victim of family or domestic violence, you are not alone. If you have succeeded in entering counseling, stay and complete the process of healing despite the pain. You have in essence embarked on a life renewal and growth-oriented process that would change your life. Counseling of the domestic violence or spousal battery survivor has two principal phases. They include:

- The emotional release or baggage excavation phase
- The self-renewal and skill acquisition phase

Emotional Release of the Survivor

As was indicated in Chapter Eight, the first therapeutic encounter with a client is for an initial intake assessment. When a survivor is first seen she may be agitated, angry, anxious, and fearful. She may exhibit visible tremors, and avoid eye contact with the counselor because of the shame and pain. For some survivors, talking to a male therapist can be difficult. Generally, the survivor turns her anger inward— thus it is quite common in the mental status examination done in the first session to find suicidal tendencies. This urge or impulse to kill herself should be taken seriously, and pursued to ascertain if she has a plan for her demise. The presence of a suicidal plan is indicative of its imminence. Homicidal ideation, in which the survivor indicates she wants to kill the perpetrator, is often more than a gesture of intent. It understandably reflects her confusion, pain, shame, and anger. The suicidal and homicidal impulses must be evaluated carefully because if they are acted upon serious repercussions can ensue. Although suicidal and homicidal features are part of the clinical profile of a survivor, a skilled counselor would know if these should be managed clinically or with the aid of law enforcement for protection.

The human mind is not a *tabula rasa* or blank slate. It is like a tape recorder. It records life's events and replay them constantly, and often without warning. The survivor has recorded within her at the conscious, pre-conscious, and unconscious levels, the agony of her emotional and physical abuse, and the rage associated with the incessant assault to her integrity and self-esteem. A major symptom of her disorder is the flashback(s), wherein vivid mental images of her battery, with the accompanying feelings (fear, anger), and emotional states (rage, anxiety, frustration, ambivalence) appear suddenly and without any emotional or behavioral warning. These flashbacks are part of the Post-Traumatic

Stress Disorder (PTSD) survivors of spousal battery are diagnosed as suffering from. Some clinicians (Walker, 1984) have used the classification Battered Women's Syndrome to describe similar and more specific symptoms exhibited by battered women. PTSD is a major anxiety disorder officially classified in the American Psychiatric Association's Diagnostic and Statistical Manual Revised—Third Edition (DSM-III-R). The DSM-III-R (1987) houses all mental, psychological, or psychiatric disorders.

Some of the major symptoms of PTSD listed in the DSM-III, and easily recognized in the spousal battery survivor include:

- Nightmares, and recurrent distressing dreams of the emotional abuse and physical battery
- The sudden feeling and acting as if the battery were recurring (illusions, hallucinations, flashbacks)
- Difficulty falling and staying asleep
- Difficulty concentrating, irritability, or outbursts of anger
- Exaggerated startle response and hypervigilance
- Avoidance of thoughts or feelings associated with the battery
- Avoidance of those activities, situations, and places that arouse memories or recollections of the spousal battery
- Feelings of detachment and estrangement from others
- Restricted emotional range such as an inability to experience love feelings
- Humiliation and feelings of helplessness
- Fears of life threatening injury
- Distressing recollections of the battery that are intrusive and recurrent

- Distressing psychological reactions when exposed to activities or events symbolizing or resembling the battery—including anniversaries of the abuse
- Repetitive play activities in which themes or aspects of the family violence are expressed by children
- Children lose developmental skills they recently acquired such as language competency; adults exhibit a grossly diminished interest in significant activities (sex, socializing, educational and career goals)
- Anxiety and depression

The clinical picture provides information for treatment planning, and sets the stage for the recovery process to begin. The counselor is aware that the survivor's behavior is a normal response to spousal battery. Equipped with this knowledge, the counselor may have to get a psychiatric examination to rule out the need for medication. The healing or recovery process is ready to begin.

Some spousal battery survivors repress the memories of their attacks; thus denying it entirely, or that significant parts of the abuse occurred. Although the repression was adaptive, and helped them to cope with the harsh and unpleasant reality of spousal battery, their continued denial exacerbates and prolongs problem resolution, and impedes the recovery process. It is a mistaken belief that deeply embedded or repressed memories of traumatic events do not negatively affect our well being. The skilled counselor assists the survivor in uncovering the traumatic memories, which in their cathartic release, an emotional purging and psychic renewal take place. Similarly, some survivors experience a painful period when they are preoccupied with the abuse. They obsessively think about it daily, and compulsively talk about it to anyone who would listen. They have flashbacks, intrusive thoughts, and nightmares. They cry incessantly, lose their appetite, shed weight, and have trouble in their daily functioning. Again, the skilled therapist places the survivor's emotional and behavioral reactions in perspective and provides meaningful assurances that she is not experiencing a psychotic breakdown, or going crazy. The counselor offers supportive psychotherapy, and uses the counseling methodologies to alleviate her problems.

As you begin the unfamiliar process of psychotherapy, you will not be able to control material stored in your long-term memory repository. By trying to repress the painful memories you will trigger anxiety, nightmares, fears, headaches, or panic attacks. Bass and Davis (1993) suggested that the survivor should relax and let the memories emerge spontaneously. They caution against using alcohol, drugs, or food to suppress these vital memories. It is important to emphasize that the batterer is not inflicting his sadistic pain on you anymore, although in your mind it may feel that way. Releasing the painful memories is a critical part of the healing process. It is not a continuation of the spousal battery.

Panic Attacks

Panic reactions are not uncommon to spousal battery survivors. These are anxiety-based physical reactions. It can be a frightening experience for the survivor every time she has an attack, but especially the first time. Panic attacks are classified under anxiety disorders. The symptoms of a panic attack include dizziness, faintness, shortness of breath, smoldering sensations, tremors or shaking, choking, sweating, nausea or abdominal pain, palpitations and increased heart rate, chest pain or discomfort, fear of going crazy, or of uncontrolled behavior, fear of dying.

The panic attack the survivor experiences seems to appear when her feelings or emotions are out of control. The smoldering sensations, palpitations, and fear of dying are real, and frightening. Your fear increases the anxiety and the symptoms become overwhelming. Panic attacks can be triggered by those repressed or deeply buried memories when they seep to the surface. This is a good reason why they should be uncovered and worked through in therapy. As counselors Ellen Bass and Laura Davis (1993) suggested, "Trying to push a memory away can also cause a panic." Events you encounter in your present circumstance have the potential of reminding you of that terrifying history of abuse, and activating a panic attack as well. Panic attacks can be dangerous because of the physical changes your body undergoes. When you sense a panic attack is imminent try to be calm, and do not scramble into action. Acting out of haste can be counterproductive. Your turbulent emotional and physical state contribute to poor judgment and decision making, and the wrong choices. If you are driving when a panic attack strikes, pull over to the side of the road and stop. If you are standing, hold on to the wall or a piece of furniture then sit as slowly as you can. Do not drink alcohol or ingest drugs to alleviate a panic attack. Panic reactions are managed medically and therapeutically. Cognitive behavior modification techniques are most commonly used with panic attacks.

Survivors are encouraged to develop a list of relaxation exercises, and other techniques to manage their panic attacks. This can best be accomplished with assistance from your therapist, particularly when you are not having a panic reaction. Some of the items on your list may include these:

- Meditation.
- Deep breathing and other relaxation exercises.
- Listening to soothing music.
- Writing fiction or non-fiction.
- Taking a hot shower or bubble bath.

- Calling members of your recovery support group.
- Stroking your pets.
- Crying and laughing appropriately.
- Watching your favorite home video.
- Solving a puzzle or playing a video game.
- Engaging in aerobic exercise.
- Thought stopping: consciously reversing your thought processes.
- Reading or reciting poetry.
- Reaching out and calling your therapist.

This is only a partial list, the reader or survivor may complete his or her own listing based on his or her specific personality constellation, or available resources. Any exercise listed must take into account the nature of a panic attack and its symptoms, so that an exercise does not further endanger the survivor.

Healing

There are three major factors mitigating change in the healing process. They include: (1) Emotional honesty about one's victimization; (2) De-escalating self-blame; and (3) Anger resolution and grieving.

To heal from spousal battery, a survivor must admit she was victimized. This is difficult because it is a self-indictment that says to the survivor and others she was weak, easily manipulative, with a dysfunctional personality. When an alcoholic is motivated to, and serious about change, he or she has to admit to being an alcoholic—that his or her life has become unmanageable. When women are battered, they learn not to trust their perceptions and judgment. They reason that if their perceptions and judgment were that good, they would not have been trapped in a spousal battery relationship. So they pretend the abuse did not happen. They deny its existence because of shame, embarrassment, and the assault to their self-esteem such an admission would create.

A survivor's confusion is exacerbated when the perpetrator minimizes, and claims repeatedly he just pushed her, he was not serious, she did not cry, or stopped him, or told him how she was feeling. So she is left unsure about what occurred. Even when the abuser, or other witnesses deny you were battered, and insist they saw or heard nothing, you have to trust your perceptions and experiences. As Bass and Davis (1993) pointed out, "Even if your memories feel too extreme to be real or too unimportant to count, you have to come to terms with the fact that someone did those things to you."

The most common defense survivors use to cope with their hurt, pain, and shame is denial. They simply pretend it did not happen. This denial is a postponement of facing and resolving their hurt, pain, and shame. However, denial does not erase the mental torment, nightmares, flashbacks, difficulty concentrating, difficulty falling and staying asleep, or other PTSD symptoms. To successfully heal, a survivor must be emotionally honest, and face her truth.

One of the most potent ways of confronting and resolving denial is in a support group of survivors, who have themselves faced and worked through their denial. These survivors would not only believe your story, they would provide you with unconditional support. The bona fide support group, whether it be for alcoholism, food addiction, bereavement, or divorced parents, is a potent source of recovery. The support fellowship effectively augments traditional forms of psychotherapy and counseling. The support group is an antidote for domestic violence, spousal abuse, or any other problem of this magnitude.

The support group has healing forces survivors and professional counselors have recognized. The group mobilizes its healing forces to assist survivors in overcoming their pain, shame and other behavioral or psychological problems. When other group participants tell their stories—the survivor—who is new to recovery, sees herself mirrored in the process. She hears their pain, senses their good intention, concern, respect, and involvement. It soon becomes contagious, and the new survivor realizes it is okay not only to listen, but speak and share as well. She begins to become comfortable with herself, and before long she finds the comfort and ease to let go of her psychological baggage free from the fear and anxiety. The positive feeling of release reinforces her self-disclosing behavior.

To heal from spousal battery, the survivor has to be emotionally honest about her psychological abuse and physical violence. Although women have been socialized to suffer in silence, and may believe that silence keeps a lid on their shame and pain, it does not, and works in favor of the batterer. The abuser may have said "If you talk I'll kill you," "no one will believe you," or "I'll deny it." If you remain silent, you are undoubtedly still under his manipulation. Breaking one's silence to speak out is often punctuated by fear, anxiety, confusion, self-doubt, and a sense of betrayal. The survivor needs to understand that loyalty was betrayed the first time the perpetrator battered her, and everytime he subsequently struck. To remain silent is to be stuck in the victim's mode. The mode of survival is healthy, and all survivors speak out. As a victim, you may have kept silent because you were embarrassed, ashamed, afraid, and blamed yourself, or felt someone would have blamed you for destroying the man, and his family. We understand that rationale even though we do not agree with it. The horrors of domestic violence and spousal battery are better known to the world today, and support is a lot more available. Even though you have learned the three S's—"silence," "shame," and "secrecy"—you can unlearn them by speaking out today. Start by disclosing this secret with someone you trust—your therapist, support group, friend, or family member.

As Ellen Bass and Laura Davis (1993) suggested, when you first disclose to someone you were abused you may simultaneously feel "terrified and relieved." You may have some reservations or self-doubts whether or not you did the correct thing. It is no doubt an unaccustomed and frightening act for the person who is new to recovery, but sharing this secret has multiple benefits according to these counselors. The benefits include:

- The survivor is emotionally honest in facing her battery.
- You open the door to receiving help.
- You are breaking through the denial to get in touch with your feelings.
- You can view your battery through the empathic eyes of a caring survivor.
- You begin the process of deeper, more meaningful and honest relations.
- You now subscribe to membership in a distinguished group of survivors, who refuse to be immobilized by shame and secrecy or suffer in silence.
- You contribute significantly to the elimination of abuse by breaking the silence in which it is allowed to thrive .
- Your actions and behavior provide a model for other spousal battery survivors.
- You gain self-assurance and self-confidence as you eventually develop a sense of pride and autonomy.

When you are able to share your secret with someone, who listens respectfully, caringly, and non-judgmentally, your pain will ease dramatically. When the survivor is able to relinquish the weight of her silence, shame, and secrecy, she sufficiently unburdens herself to begin the introspective search deep within. This internal exploration helps you to get in touch with the lost self, that vital part of your being, which was subordinated and neglected because you catered to and were dominated by the batterer. You are now free from his grip, if you can only allow yourself to believe this. Some therapists (Bradshaw, 1988) have described our "inner child" as the feelings of hurt and pain we carry within from our childhood days. Although they are deeply buried, they still function and affect our lives. We cannot fully heal if we resist and fail to get in contact with how this aspect of our past affects our life.

> When you aren't in touch with the younger parts of yourself, you are missing a vital part of who you are. When you hate the child inside you, you hate parts of yourself. When you take care of the child inside, you learn to nurture yourself (Bass and Davis, 1993).

When a survivor gets in touch with the "inner child," she begins to hear her pain, face the brutality of her abuse, and confront the childlike dependency fostered in the spousal battery relationship. On the positive side her rewards can be prodigious and incalculable.

Grief, Anger, and Forgiveness

As a survivor in recovery you must allow yourself to go through the grieving process. Your grief will focus on the betrayal of your trust, and exploitation of your vulnerability by the man you trusted, had confidence in, and shared intimately with. Your grief will encompass the protection he denied you, the pain he inflicted on you, and the joyful or blissful relationship you were denied. Your grief will include the isolation from friends and family, and the lies you told to deceive and cover up. You must grieve for not having the ideal relationship, and all the broken promises. The grieving process will have you reflect, face the poor choices you made in picking an abusive man, and staying as long as you have. Finally, you will grieve for the time, money, effort, and pain it will take to heal. Your inability to trust, or to take risks will be part of the grieving process. The postponement of your grief is the continued harnessing of toxins in your system. Unresolved grief suffocates healthy psychological growth and psychic expression. It stifles the ability to feel and express cheer, joy, and gaiety. An inability to grieve is regressive in that it mimics the survivor's childhood years when she was not allowed to express her thoughts and feelings. The need to hide one's feelings as a child either through fear of disapproval or punishment is expressed as having been experienced by many survivors. The grieving process allows the survivor to re-live these negative experiences with caring, understanding, and supportive survivors, and/or therapists, who help facilitate her recovery.

Anger is an appropriate response to spousal battery. Many survivors may have been taught that a woman should not become angry or express her hostility. Some survivors may be afraid to become angry because they have lost control in the past and became violent. In their family of origin, and in subsequent relationships, the survivor may have been frightened by the destructive force of anger out of control. As a result, the survivor may have learned to hide, avoid, or bury her anger. She may have suffocated her anger to avoid taking revenge on the batterer. Unresolved or repressed anger devours its victims, and seeps into their behavior unknowingly. We addressed anger and its deleterious effects in Chapter Eight. However, when a survivor feels anger, she has many options available for its release or expression. Feeling and appropriately expressing the anger she experiences for the batterer would not invalidate her growth or the therapeutic gains she has made. A survivor can be infuriated by the batterer's violent and exploitative behavior without losing her dignity as a person. If she responds to the batterer with violence and abuse, manipulation and exploitation, she would have successfully managed to stoop to his despicable level of indignity.

If the survivor does not get in touch with her anger, resolve it to an appreciable degree, it can take charge and control her behavior, with disastrous consequences. It can be displaced onto innocent individuals such as children. Anger, like positive stress, "is a necessary and, at times, a positive life force. It can be an impetus for change, growth, and adaptation" (McKenzie, 1988). Many survivors have positively used their anger to sever their ties to emotionally abusive and physically violent relationships. Some have used their anger to enter and remain in treatment.

Others have become sufficiently angry to divorce their abusive spouse or leave battering boyfriends, and challenge sexually harassing bosses legally. Some of the constructive ways of resolving anger include:

- Get in touch with your anger, and recognize its source.

- Use your cognitive skills to think of constructive or appropriate ways to release your anger.

- Talk through your angry feelings with the source—person or persons associated (see Assertiveness Skills in Chapter Ten).

- Postpone confronting the source of your anger until you are sufficiently calm.

- If you cannot confront the source directly get an intermediary.

- Speak to others about your abuse.
- Talk to your therapist or support group.
- Make daily entries in your diary or journal.
- Take an assertiveness or self-defense course.
- Organize to change the anti-women sentiments and laws.
- Organize a political march or seminar on domestic violence.
- Talk to your spouse about your anger.
- Screaming in the appropriate place can be a first-step release of anger.

The reader or survivor can generate a longer list of anger management techniques. Work with your counselor to develop a list of other techniques. The release and working through of your anger can be the first creative step to a more healthy lifestyle.

Forgiveness of Self

Sometimes the harshest judge of her behavior, and the one to identify character defects in herself is the survivor. From the survivor's self-condemnation, we can easily see how exceedingly well she has learned from the batterer. The forgiveness I am addressing is inner-directed for you, the survivor. The only one you are required to forgive is yourself. Your shame, self-blame, self-condemnation, and disapproval for the coping behaviors you employed under those horrible conditions will not fully evaporate unless you forgive yourself. Forgiveness involves giving up the resentment, animosity, bitterness, hatred, hostility, outrage, vexation, and repulsion you harbor for the perpetrator. Your holding on to these creates a prolonged state of tension that erodes and takes its toll on your psychological and physical well-being.

Forgiveness of self entails being lenient and compassionate toward yourself so that all your energies and motivation can be directed toward the healing process. Forgiveness is not acquiescence or giving up. It is not a substitute for problem exploration and resolution. Forgiveness is vital because it complements or augments the process of change. Forgiveness does not mean forgetness. Survivors who can come to terms with their abuse such that it is acknowledged as having occurred will find that forgiveness and compassion usher in a sense of self-realization, autonomy, and immunity.

Notice I have said very little if anything about the perpetrator in the forgiveness of self. Many survivors mistakenly believe that to adequately resolve their problems and sufficiently repair, they have to seek and receive forgiveness from the batterer. Some survivors, to appease their conscience and ease their guilt, pursue the perpetrator for his forgiveness. These behaviors are clearly idiosyncratic and dysfunctional. These acts of seeking the batterer's forgiveness are residual feelings that are tantamount to re-entering the spousal battery relationship. Many battered women express some pity for the batterer; others assert a need to reconcile the negative and positive feelings they harbor for him. If the resolution of a survivor's ambivalent feelings can be found in compassion or forgiveness, only she, and her counselor, or support group is at liberty to say.

Essential Ingredients of Change

Therapeutic change involves a shift from one's original identity, with the substitution of different modes of perceiving and thinking, processing emotions, and behaving.

- Motivation—motivation is the intrinsic drive to change. Without it, internal commitment, and subsequent change are difficult if not impossible to achieve. One who is motivated to change for others is in essence failure bound.

- Awareness and Insight—awareness is the sense that something is missing or not quite functional in one's life. Insight is a deeper level of awareness that informs individuals how a missing element of their behavior, or the dysfunctional behavior itself affects them and others negatively (or positively). Whereas awareness indicates you are in an unhealthy relationship, insight tells you how and why you make poor choices in mates, what needs you are fulfilling, and what the emotional consequences are likely to be.

Tenacity—behavioral dysfunctions and personality disorders develop over considerable time. There is generally the unrealistic expectation when individuals enter therapy that instant change or a quick fix will result. Psychological and behavioral changes are slow processes especially when problems are deep-seated, and have existed for some time. However, counseling and psychotherapy have become more intensified and short-term in recent years. Survivors must be patient and tenacious. Every small step contributes to significant lifestyle changes. Old habits are often resistant to change, and things seem to get worse before they improve. The survivor has to be determined and stay the therapeutic course.

Repetition—learning in general, and particularly for behavioral change, requires repetition. The constant processing and reprocessing of new information are involved on the cognitive or thinking, emotional or feeling, and behavioral levels. This intense level of involvement can be tiring and discouraging. Think of other activities (driving, academic pursuits, tennis or golf) that require repetition before mastery is achieved. Most of the growth-oriented changes we undertake in life are by design, repetitious. Here again, the survivor has to stay on course.

Anxiety and Fear

Anxiety is an uncomfortable state, and fear can be a frightening feeling. When they are combined, the individual may choose to run, hide, or both. Anxiety and fear can be used positively to motivate a survivor to work hard for meaningful change. Growth and change can be achieved despite the presence of anxiety and fear. Counselors have proven techniques to reduce anxiety and fear. Share what you are experiencing with your counselor, work them through instead of using them as impediments to your growth.

T and R Balance—therapeutic activities are important for your re-socialization and growth. If you become so immersed in individual and group therapy that you attend support groups, and choose for your leisure reading counseling material as well—you may be too saturated therapeutically. T and R refer to the therapeutic and recreational balance in your life. Do not be compulsive or addictive in your therapeutic endeavors. Make sure you have a balance in your life, or you will burnout therapeutically in a short time. Have a non-therapeutic group of friends as well.

Need Fulfillment Behaviors

The survivor comes to the realization at some point that she needs to make changes in her life on many levels. As you begin to learn how to fulfill your needs in functional ways, and in the process develop healthier needs, it becomes easier to relinquish the old dysfunctional behaviors. When these occur, your self-confidence, self-esteem, and self-image will improve as well. Do not sabotage your growth because the new ways of thinking, feeling, and behaving feel uncomfortable.

Self-Praise and Self-Reinforcement

Therapeutic change can be difficult, frustrating, complex, and painful. Success may be elusive at first, and quite infrequent even later on. When you have a success, tap yourself on the shoulder, celebrate and relish your accomplishment. You deserve to be treated positively for your hard work. Self-praise and self-reinforcement are your rewards. Continue your commendable work.

Self-Condemnation

Failure has its price. Often, the price is a self-inflicted wound by the survivor herself. When a survivor relapses, and the old behaviors predominate again, however briefly, she may engage in self-condemnation. She may call herself derogatory names, similar or identical to those she may have been called by the batterer. She may drink excessively, over-eat, or otherwise punish herself. Relapse is an unavoidable part of growth and change. Use your relapse to re-motivate, re-direct, and re-energize yourself for harder work. Do not terminate the change processes. When you have a relapse, appropriately mourn or feel bad, but forgive yourself and move on. Remember you are in a learning mode, and mistakes are inevitable.

Taking Charge of Your Life

The change process cannot be rushed. You may feel an urgency to get on with your life, and others may prod you along in response to their own impatience. If you artificially rush the process as a way of escaping from the hurt, then you are emotionally dishonest, sabotaging the healing process, and reverting to the old dysfunctional behaviors. The more you are able to work the treatment plan with your therapist, focus on your counseling goals, follow treatment recommendations fully and without any deviation, the closer and quicker you will achieve success. Success is the removal or working through of a survivor's rage, anger, hatred, betrayal, pain or hurt, and other psychological and behavioral problems. Success is the achievement of a sense of inner tranquility, self-respect, and self-efficacy or personal effectiveness. It is futuristic regarding the survivor's acquired ability to be assertive, make healthier choices in her life, gain self-confidence, and have more autonomy. Taking charge of your life means designing an agenda unilaterally or collaboratively with your counselor, and working as hard as you can to achieve all the stated goals. Many survivors, reluctantly or enthusiastically, enter counseling with tremendous pain, shame, low self-confidence, injured self-esteem, and a poor self-image. Psychological repair as gained from the healing process offers more than the cessation of pain and elimination of shame. The healing process, if followed through, is a gift of life.

As the survivor heals, she develops a more objective perspective on her environment, and the place she occupies in it. She gains an intrinsic valuing of her strengths and weaknesses. She learns that she is a valuable human being despite how she treats herself, and is treated by others. The survivor learns that letting go of her psychological and behavioral baggage is the best valuing of herself she can claim. The survivor's valuing of herself is seen in her development of inner directive skills, and attitudes of interdependence, creative thoughts, and the emotional flexibility (Blocher, 1974).

How Effective is your Therapist?

When survivors enter into a counseling relationship, the therapeutic contract addresses the expectations that they will be treated with respect, not harmed or exploited, and offered the best methodology available for change. The survivor entrusts her vulnerabilities, insecurities, fears, shame and pain to a stranger, whose competence she has no skill to evaluate. What minimum competencies should we require of counselors who work with domestic or spousal battery survivors? The presence of these skill areas can facilitate a survivor's recovery and growth:

- **Education and Training**

    Domestic violence and spousal battery were America's "dirty secret" for decades, consequently, mainstream educational institutions did not teach counseling skills in these areas. Counselors who work with survivors must educate themselves in the dynamics, intervention, and healing processes of domestic violence and spousal abuse.

- **Examine your Biases and Assumptions**

    Do not treat the survivor as a victim. The therapeutic process can be contaminated with disrespect, stereotypes, and blaming if the counselor has not worked through his or her gender-biases, negative assumptions and evaluations about battered women. As was noted earlier, a battered woman has successfully made the transition from victim to survivor when she distances herself from the abuse, seeks, and successfully completes treatment. Counselors will not be effective if they unload their baggage in the therapeutic milieu. They must resolve their biases and other baggage before attempting to assist the survivor.

Spousal Battery Treatment Hierarchy

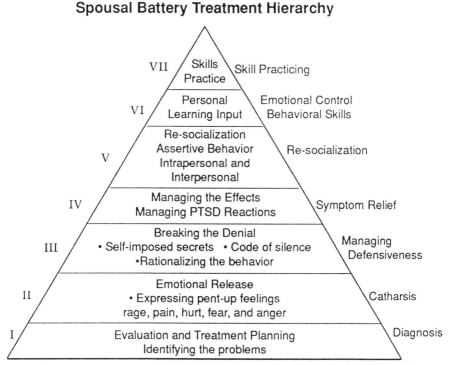

The Spousal Battery Treatment Hierarchy depicts seven critical areas involved in the therapeutic transition from victim to survivor.

- **Validate the Survivor and her Feelings**

    Irrespective of a survivor's functional or dysfunctional behavior, she has the intrinsic value as a person. The survivor, who has endured horrible experiences, needs to be validated as a person. Her feelings of fear and anger, and experiences of shame and pain are legitimate and should be unconditionally validated.

These feelings and experiences are natural and genuine responses to the horror of domestic violence.

Verbal, sexual, and other aspects of physical abuse have debilitating effects on battered women. Counselors must recognize and acknowledge these through their verbal and non-verbal behavior. Validation of the survivor also means believing her story even when her memory seems unreliable.

- **Empathize with the Survivor not her Batterer**

   Whether well-intentioned, inadvertent, or other-wise, the mention of and empathy for the perpetrator is insulting to the victim and anti-therapeutic. Counselors are expected to show loyalty to their clients.

- **Know your Limitations**

   Not all counselors are equipped to manage psychiatric emergencies. The need for medication, management of psychotic reactions, homicidal and suicidal tendencies are eventualities a counselor must act on by referral to the appropriate professionals. Additionally, when individual therapy is complemented by the support group fellowship, the survivor has a greater chance for successful outcome, with a very good prognosis.

- **Authentic means to be Real**

   There is a phenomenon in therapy called congruency. It means that when therapists are being phony, unreal, or inauthentic, they are transparent, and the client sees through that artificiality. So if a counselor is angry, but is trying to fake otherwise, the client notices it. The discrepancy between what one feels and expresses is emotional dishonesty. Once the client uncovers this deception, the counselor loses credibility and effectiveness as a helper, mentor or model, and teacher. If as a counselor you have feelings of disgust, fury, and outrage, or empathy for the survivor's shame and pain, you must find an appropriate way to convey them. Take the risk and self-disclose instead of trying to conceal them. We must always be prepared to set an example by doing that which we require of our clients. The major requirement in a counselor's self-disclosure is that it be for the benefit of the survivor, and not obscure what she says or is actively resolving.

Survivors heal yourselves—at your own pace—and in your own time—but do not procrastinate.

Chapter Ten

The Empowered Survivor

The empowered woman is a self-directed individual, who rejects abuse and accepts survival on her own healthy terms. Empowerment grants permanent permission for a survivor to begin living assertively—unencumbered by the pain of her past.

V. Michael McKenzie, Ph.D.

Empowered survivors have learned to value themselves as capable human beings, who possess the emotional freedom to feel love, joy, anger, or fear without requiring or asking for permission. Empowered survivors have sufficiently healed to say no to spousal battery without guilt, self-blame, self-condemnation, or apologies. Empowered survivors make no excuses for feeling good and positive, or rejecting abuse of themselves and their children.

Empowerment is both a process and an outcome. The process of empowerment involves the development of self-awareness and insight, knowledge of one's social environment, and skills for effective communication and interpersonal functioning. The outcome phase of empowerment comprises of the following:

- Survivor develops an armamentarium of assertive behaviors.

- Survivor develops a theory or method for detecting and correcting her problem behaviors, and making healthy or functional choices.

- Survivor sets realistic goals and evaluates their effectiveness.

An empowered survivor gains and exhibits self-confidence. She becomes self-assured, inner-directed and focused. She learns to solve her problems instead of avoiding them and procrastinating. She engages in less self-condemnation, and is more tolerant of her frailties, fallibilities, mistakes, and failures. The empowered survivor is constructive in her self-criticism, compassionate, and self-appreciative. She works diligently and consistently to reduce and eliminate self-defeating and sabotaging behaviors, and other negativistic tendencies. The empowered woman's optimism and motivation are grounded in realistic goals, and backed by sustained efforts to change. The empowered woman has acquired an authentic sense of independence, and values the power and control she has over her own life. She does not dominate others. She does not relinquish the power and control over her life to anyone. She understands that the transition from victim to survivor is not a magical phenomenon; it requires consistent effort, therapeutic guidance, and independent practice.

Assertiveness Training

<pre>
                        Passive
                       Aggressive
Passive   _____   Aggressive
Behavior   Assertiveness   Behavior
</pre>

The Assertive Behavior Continuum

The feminist movement is credited with increasing women's awareness that they have more rights than were previously ascribed or given to them. In recent years, the behavior therapy technique known as assertiveness training has taught women how to harness their newly defined rights. The emotional and hysterical outbursts associated with some women have been transformed into a realistic image of self-confidence and self-assurance. Those women who were previously silent sufferers have become vocal in their attempts to fulfill their needs. As a survivor becomes assertive, she sheds the old image of dependent victim, and redefines herself as a capable, and self-directed person.

Passive Behavior

The *Webster's Dictionary* (1987) defines passive as "receiving or enduring without resistance." "Submissive." "Existing or occurring without being active, open, or direct." The battered woman or victim of domestic violence is, with few exceptions, a passive person. The passive victim is often a silent sufferer, who is inept at fighting back, or finds excuses for avoiding and not confronting the batterer. Passive means submissive, compliant, obedient, unresisting, allowing advantage to be taken, indifferent, fearful, inert, idle, and afraid to fight back. Passive behavior is self-reinforcing. The more a woman refuses to fight back or represent herself, the more passive she becomes. Passive behavior is unhealthy; it invites others to exploit the victim. The hurt, resentment, anger, frustration and pain that develop when a victim passively allows herself to be exploited often reach explosive levels within. These pent up emotions can exacerbate hypertension, heart disease, or other cardiovascular disorders. Additionally, the hostilities that build up within the passive person are expressed through displacement unto innocent and less threatening individuals. Passive behavior allows other people to satisfy their needs at the expense of the passive person.

Passive-Aggressive Behavior

Passive aggressive behavior is another counterproductive way of responding to a perpetrator's dominance, exercise of power and control. The passive aggressive response is an indirect way of releasing anger, and other hostilities. It does not effectively communicate a person's disapproval and dissatisfaction with the behavior of another. A passive aggressive response to provocation may include self-mutilation, displaced anger resulting in attacks on children or pets, or slamming and kicking of doors. Passive-aggressive behavior does not address one's anger, hurt, irritation, or pain in a healthy manner. It is an inappropriate externalizing of emotions that does not address the source of the problem thus issues remain unsolved.

Aggressive Behavior

Behavior that attacks, denigrates, humiliates, and dominates, with the intent to win, is designated as aggressive. Aggressive behavior involves satisfying one's needs at the expense of others. Aggressive behavior is valued in many contexts, such as sales, journalism, and business. However, an aggressive posture as in all interpersonal relationships is usually an attempt to influence and shape behavior, dominate and control, and wield power. The intent in aggressive behavior generally is an infringement on the rights of others, with an outcome that is unequal.

Assertiveness

The assertive woman learns to represent herself, and express her preferences and rights in a direct and emotionally honest way. The survivor distances herself from the submissive posture that maintains dependency, and other forms of helplessness characterized by passive behavior. She disdains the attacking and aggressive persona, which results in win-lose outcomes that demolishes an opponent. The assertive survivor manages her own emotions, chooses not to dominate or control others, sets her own agenda and standards, enjoys her own company, knows how to communicate directly and openly, and is able to leave abusive relationships.

The assertive woman understands the emotional and behavioral price she paid for her previous reluctance or inability to communicate her feelings directly and openly. Her fears of being rejected, or hurting someone's feelings impeded her expression. The assertive woman learns to stop taking emotional responsibility for everyone else. She learns to put her interests first more in a self-preserving than egocentric way. While childhood learning patterns have left many women with deficient or poor interpersonal habits, assertiveness training re-teaches and re-socializes the survivor. Assertive behavior is the appropriate and functional mode of response a survivor is taught, and encouraged to use. Assertive behavior meets the needs of a survivor, without infringing on the rights of others. Assertive behavior, or simply assertiveness gives one the right to be confrontive, direct, candid, and emotionally honest with her feelings. Assertiveness entitles a survivor to make her mistakes, fail, or succeed without apologies, explanations, defensiveness, or fear of rejection.

The assertive survivor has a much healthier mode of communicating and interacting than either the passive or aggressive personality. She takes responsibility for her thoughts, feelings, and actions. There is an absence of game-playing in assertive behavior. The assertive survivor has in effect chosen to be a mature adult in her behavior. These are the four major components of assertive behavior (Le Mon, 1990; Paris and Casey, 1983).

- The assertive survivor expresses what she is thinking and feeling directly and spontaneously.
- The assertive survivor does not apologize for express-ing her emotions and thoughts honestly.
- The assertive survivor refuses to be manipulated by the shame or guilt-inducing behavior of others when she communicates.
- The assertive survivor does not infringe on the rights of others in achieving her goals.

The Three Stages of Assertive Problem-Solving

1. Confrontation — Confrontation involves the uninhib-ited expression of negative evaluations or criticisms, dis-appointment, displeasure, anger, or fear. The use of con-frontational skills allows a survivor to vent her strong emotions constructively as opposed to repressing them. The mastery of confrontational skills permits the individual an immediate and nonviolent resolution of internal conflict and interpersonal disputes.

In initiating a confrontation, it is critical not to demean or attack the individual. This non-facilitating behavior can create defensiveness. Defensiveness in one or both partici-pants can impede the conflict resolution process. The most effective way to begin resolving an interpersonal dispute is to clearly and openly state the emotional and behavioral effects the conflict has on an affected party. Verbal attacks do not facilitate the confrontational mode. The following steps illustrate the confrontational process:

- Maintain a calm demeanor, and ask to speak with the person privately and confidentially about an issue that is very important to you. Be specific about how much time you are requesting.

- Without being trivial, superficial, or artificial, say something complimentary or positive to and about the person you are to address. A positive remark sets a tone of cordiality, and acts as an emotional regulator.

- Tell the listener directly, honestly, and non-attackingly what aspects of his verbal and/or non-verbal behavior have affected you and how. Be specific. Be non-judgmental and describe the behavior without insults or name-calling. Be brief and non-punitive, but provide a full account of what disturbs you.

- Ask the listener if he or she would verbally reflect back his or her understanding of your complaint or issue of contention. Check for accuracy in what you said, and what the listener heard. Make appropriate corrections.

- Ask for the listener's reactions to what you presented including his or her feelings. Listen without interruption. Request behavioral changes if none are spontaneously offered. Explore options and offer suggestions if asked.

- Bring closure by thanking the person for having accorded you the opportunity to share your feelings, issues, or concerns. Thank the listener for listening.

2. Accepting Feedback — After the confrontation has been initiated, the confronter has an obligation to listen to the respondent in a non-defensive manner. The confronter should resist defending him or herself, offering explanations, making demands, or issuing threats. He or she should engage in active or reflective listening. The following are major tenets of assertive listening:

- Maintain a calm demeanor and actively listen to what the person has to say.

- Ask for clarification or elaboration if you do not understand what was said without judging or attacking the person's communication style.

- Constructive communication involves an interchange in which two interlocutors respectfully talk and listen in turn. Unauthorized or unsolicited interruptions are impolite and disrespectful. They generate frustration.

- Share with the individual that you understand what was said. Include the person's feelings if they were expressed or are easily identifiable. Use such words as "it seems" or "appears" thus allowing room to validate or invalidate your observations.

- Ask if the person has any expectations regarding responses he or she wants from you.

- Respectfully ask if you may offer your reactions, feelings, perspective, or to simply tell your side.

- Own your feelings; agree to disagree. Avoid finger-pointing, and parent-child communication patterns. Resist blaming and shaming. These are self-promoting and egocentric, with the devastating results of communication breakdown and withdrawal.

Resolution or Working It Out

The final stage in assertive problem-solving involves working things out or finding a resolution. The skill steps are as follows:

- Project and maintain a calm and positive demeanor.

- Listen attentively to the other person's response, and collaboratively clarify the problem.

- Generate and evaluate options or possible solutions, with a win-win outcome in mind. Continue processing until a solution or remedy is found.

- Adopt a mutually satisfying or agreed-upon solution.

- Finalize the agreement by ensuring each party is fully aware of the solution and its ramifications.

- Plan how the solution will be implemented. Finally, agree on an evaluation method and a specified time to assess how well the solution has worked (Hammond and Yung, 1991; Richards, 1988).

A victim may increase her chances of survival if she learns and uses assertive behavior early and effectively in an abusive relationship. Many batterers would balk at a victim who attempted to engage them assertively. They are likely to intensify their abuse and physical violence. However, a woman should set her standards of acceptable behavior irrespective of how the batterer or potential abuser reacts.

Guidelines for Assertive Behavior

When you begin to assert yourself, be clear about what your specific goals are. Are you attempting to appease the other person, or just trying to prove how capable you are? Do you recognize a need to honestly express strong negative emotions, and simultaneously make the person aware what behaviors you will not tolerate? Assertive behavior requires giving up hidden agendas, game-playing, and the self-defeating aspect of one's persona. Bona fide assertive behavior facilitates communication and healthy growth. Its goals are designed to enhance interpersonal relationships.

- When the assertive survivor expresses refusals, she must communicate a decisive "no," or "I will not." Sharing why you are refusing is appropriate, but apologies are counterproductive. When applicable, you may offer the other individual an option or suggest a different course of action.

- When the assertive survivor comments on another person's behavior, she will find "I — statements" to be effective. For example, "John, when you cursed and called me names, I felt angry and belittled." When applicable, offer suggestions for alternative behavior. For instance, "John, I have no problem accepting negative comments about my behavior. I would appreciate if you didn't curse or use insults and put-downs when you talk to me."

- An assertive survivor makes good eye contact by looking the person straight in the eye when talking or listening. She is also aware of her own body language, and recognizes signs of hesitancy, indirectness, lack of self-confidence and self-assurance. For example, poor eye contact, slumped shoulders, a hand over her mouth, shuffling feet, and other body distractions reduce the effectiveness of assertive behavior. Monitor your voice tone and inflection. Inaudible whispers or overly-loud tones are ineffective communication styles.

- When you express anger, annoyance, disappointment, or criticism, focus your comments on the person's overt behavior. Resist engaging in attacks, judgment, personality evaluations, character assassinations, or guessing at the motivation behind the other person's behavior.

- The assertive survivor must insist on being treated respectfully, with fairness and justice. Request an explanation when you are asked to do something unjust or unreasonable. Insist on being heard; give prompt and brief replies without being interrupted.

- Passive, passive aggressive, and unassertive behaviors are learned, and can be un-learned. As you begin to behave more assertively, fear, anxiety, and other types of discomfort will be experienced. Persevere, and do not abandon your assertive responses. It takes time and practice to think, feel, and behave in the effective way your prefer.

- In thinking assertively, work on replacing your anger, fear, anxiety, shame-eliciting and guilt-ridden thoughts with more adaptive, growth-enhancing, and calm-producing ones.

- In making the transition from passive to assertive, work on less anxiety-provoking situations first. Do not tackle the major issues or most anxiety-laden situations in the beginning. The major emotionally laden problems may defeat your goal of changing through small incremental steps.

- Make daily or weekly entries of your assertive-behavior responses in a log. Review them regularly, and have evaluative discussions with a close friend—incorporate any valuable feedback. Observe good models.

- Do not be discouraged by or punish yourself for behaving aggressively or non-assertively. Instead, evaluate where you digressed from your plan, and devise ways to get back on track. You can always improve your assertive behavior at the next opportunity.

- Finally, reward yourself in that very special way when you motivate yourself to give an assertive response. Whether or not you get the desired response from the other person, reward yourself for the effort (Wolfe, 1976).

One of the major rewards that awaits the assertive survivor is her Bill of Rights. Her transition from victim to survivor is testimony to endurance and hard work. These rights are part of our basic human rights, and should not have to be fought for. Assertive behavior begins with the implicit assumption that every human being has basic unconditional rights that are not contingent on status or performance. The assertive survivor may extend her Bill of Rights to include any additional rights she deems important.

Assertive Behavior

Bill of Rights

1. The right to be treated with dignity and respect.
2. The right to express your thoughts and feelings without threats or intimidation.
3. The right to change your mind.
4. The right to say "no" without feeling guilty.
5. The right to set your own priorities.
6. The right to insist on fair and equal treatment.
7. The right to be listened to and taken seriously.
8. The right to ask for what you want.
9. The right to think and talk about yourself in a positive way.
10. The right not to accept responsibility for others.
11. The right to be wrong or right.
12. The right to be human and assume full responsibility for your decisions and behavior.
13. The right to judge your thoughts and behavior.
14. The right to feel comfortable expressing and accepting complements.
15. The right to refuse sexual advances without being attacked verbally and physically.
16. The right to choose your own friends.
17. The right to be yourself without the embellishments others have designed.

The transition from victim to survivor can be exciting because of the growth potential and increased learning that can take place. The following areas are essential for the survivor's adjustment.

Self-Esteem

As one of the basic psychological needs, self-esteem is an important part of healthy human development. Its absence can retard the psychological development of young and old alike. It is often confused with negative self-appraisal, the obsessive and compulsive need to be perfect, and the narcissistic injuries that leave us feeling empty, disappointed, angry or depressed. Self-esteem is a complex phenomenon, with many features that include self-worth and self-confidence. Our weakness and resilience in response to failure and other negative experiences, our self-image and self-efficacy, and our sense of belonging are part of self-esteem. In essence, positive self-esteem has two major parts: Self-worth and self-efficacy. Self-worth involves those positive psychological underpinnings like self-fulfillment, success and achievement, interpersonal relationships, love, self-confidence, and a positive attitude about joyful and happy living. Self-efficacy is our competence—the energy, force, and ability to think, process, gain skills, set and achieve goals, and engage in decision-making.

High levels of positive self-esteem stimulate, motivate, and challenge us to make constructive decisions, set realistic goals, and deploy the resources necessary for attaining our goals. Whereas, low self-esteem is un-stimulating, un-motivating, such that the individual stays unchallenged with the safe and familiar, which in effect cripples self-esteem. The healthier our self-esteem, the more capable we are of withstanding or coping with the vicissitudes of life. Good, solid, or healthy self-esteem helps women to surmount obstacles in the workplace, or overcome setbacks in relationships free of the emotional devastation to which many succumb. Healthy self-esteem does not permit the kind of dysfunction in which a woman would avoid intimacy or compromise her principles to guard her ego against hurt or rejection at any cost to her self-respect. High self-esteem is self-renewing, self-reinforcing, and self-rewarding.

Very often high self-esteem is positively correlated with ambition, achievement in career aspirations and emotional, intellectual, cognitive, romantic, and spiritual growth. The higher the level of self-esteem we have, the greater our expression of contentment, richness, and inner satisfaction. The lower our self-esteem the more dubious and evasive we are, and the more we play emotionally dishonest games to prove our self-worth, which is only artificial. Positive self-esteem facilitates open, honest, and unpretentious communication, and steers us into healthy non-toxic relationships. Self-confident women attract and are attracted to self-confident partners. Women with positive self-esteem develop clear boundaries of appropriate behavior they accept from men. They make it clear that maltreatment is unacceptable, and, despite human frailties, they do not tolerate physical or psychological, verbal or non-verbal abuse for any reason. The self-esteemed woman clearly asks for what she wants and expresses her worthiness for respect, affection and genuine equality. Genuine self-esteem resides in the core of human personality. It is the self-confidence that radiates internally, and the self-image that glows externally making us confident, secure, and well adjusted (Branden, 1992).

If the experts are correct in their assertion that success is twenty percent aptitude and eighty percent attitude, it is not difficult to grasp why our positive mental state, positive attitude, positive behavior, and optimistic outlook on life are the key to personal and career success. Irrespective of your intelligence quotient, level of skill, competence, or ambition, poor self- esteem can derail or defeat your goals. Poor self-esteem can rob you of the gratification to be derived from the fruits of your labor. Good self-esteem, however, is the foundation or spine of healthy emotional and behavioral expression. Self-esteem represents an authentic valuing and caring for yourself as a human being. Self-esteem is not the unhealthy narcissistic self-absorption of the batterer, or the victim, who caters to others in a self-sacrificial way. Healthy self-esteem means you do love and accept yourself as a valued person. Healthy self-esteem answers this question affirmatively? Are you earnestly working to fully realize your potential; your goals and dreams; to recognize and appreciate yourself as a human being; your strengths and weaknesses, limitations and best attributes, and your accomplishments— be they small, large, or moderate? Self-esteem is the psychological channel through which your goals, aspirations, desires and wants are transformed into real, tangible, and achievable results. It also includes the capacity to be gratified, feel good, and enjoy your successes without dysfunctional excesses. Self-esteem includes the ability to reorganize and recover from failure, defeat, or disappointment without incapacitating or debilitating anxiety, fear, detachment or abandonment.

Parental Self-Esteem Building Skills

The building of self-esteem is a process, that, like personality development, goes through stages. Since the child is not developmentally capable of self-instruction, it is the caretakers or parents' responsibility to teach and help the youngster develop self-esteem. There are some conditions that are critical in the development of self-esteem, they complement each other, and the absence of one or two may be detrimental to the acquisition of healthy self-esteem.

1. Safe Environment — An environment of physical and psychological violence, verbal or non-verbal abuse is harmful to the development of healthy self-esteem. When a child is nurtured in a safe environment he or she develops trust, a sense of security, and an autonomous self-exploratory personality that enhances self-confidence. When the child succeeds at doing a task or is praised for trying or accomplishing a goal his or her self-esteem is enhanced.

2. Psychological Safety — When a youngster stumbles or fails, and he or she receives parental encouragement rather than condemnation or put-downs, the child is not likely to feel ashamed or discouraged, but instead, he or she may sense it is okay to make mistakes. He or she internalizes the message that it is okay to try until one succeeds. A sense of self-confidence, caring, and a humanness that fosters good self-esteem generally develops in these youngsters.

3. Self-Confident Personality — The human personality is the sum of all psychological and behavioral characteristics. Thus, the cumulative effects of positive experiences build a high level of tolerance for frustration, delayed gratification, constructive risk-taking, and a valued sense of competence. The negative experiences, however, remind us of the need for perseverance, and the possibilities for growth that failure does provide.

4. Affiliation or Isolation — Failure, negative self-evaluation and self-condemnation can breed shame and isolation for some individuals. However, success seems to generate self-acceptance, closeness or affiliation with others, interdependence, and a network of connectedness. Children who evaluate failure in a self-condemning way need to be encouraged to look at failure as a learning experience that is capable of generating positive growth.

5. A Sense of Autonomy — A child who has been allowed to fail without psychological or physical penalty, and whose successes are positively reinforced rather than minimized or ignored, learns healthy coping skills, inner self-confidence, resiliency, and an ability to surmount obstacles free from mental paralysis.

Bolstering Self-confidence

They came by train, bus, car, subway, and on foot. The brightly lit faces, with warm smiles that betrayed their anxiety and intimidation, were of the adolescent females who participated in the First Annual Take Our Daughters to Work Day sponsored by the Ms. Foundation. The idea was developed as a method of bolstering the self-confidence and self-esteem of adolescent girls ages nine through fifteen. Social scientists have suggested that in our gender-biased society where women have traditionally been discouraged from many professions, girls have to be reminded how competent they can become beginning with exposure to the unlimited professions open to them. *Time* magazine hosted forty-three of these young women, who participated in editorial meetings, watched art directors at their creative best, and interacted with marketing staff at work. The experience was rewarding not only for the visitors, but staff members as well. This is a very creative way to foster ambition, aspirations, goal-setting, and a host of other correlates of self-esteem. It was a positive experience for America's young women (*Time*, May 10, 1993).

Fostering Self-Confidence in Young Women

Research findings suggest that working mothers positively influence their children such that their youngsters develop high levels of self-esteem and more egalitarian gender-role attitudes and behavior. Similarly, a 1988 study of kindergarten youngsters in Washington, D.C., conducted by the School of Social Work at Smith College, found that children, whose mothers identified themselves as feminists, were "more independent, active, aggressive, strong, and unafraid." Furthermore, this study indicated that pro-feminist fathers contributed to higher self-esteem in their daughters and sons. If the goal is to raise young women and men who are emotionally healthy, intra-personally and inter-personally competent, self-confident and happy, with high levels of self-esteem and a sound self-image, parents will have to incorporate pertinent research findings in their parenting repertoire.

As young girls grow and mature, their self-confidence, self-esteem, and ability to project into the future decrease. The precipitous decline is most pronounced between the elementary and middle school years according to the 1992 study titled, *How Schools Short-Change Girls*. The study, which was conducted by the American Association of University Women (AAUW) Educational Foundation, surveyed 3,000 youngsters nationwide spanning grades four through ten. Another of its significant findings was that the self-esteem of Euro-American elementary school students was comparatively much lower (55 percent) than African-American (65 percent) or Latina youngsters (68 percent). Asian American and Native American students were not studied. As they enter middle school, the self-esteem levels of these students dipped to a meager 29 percent for Euro-Americans, 59 percent for African-Americans, and 54 percent for Latinas. Finally in their high school years, African-American female students had a self-esteem level of 58 percent, Latinas dropped to 30 percent, and Euro-Americans recorded the lowest level of 22 percent. One plausible theory that was advanced to explain these self-esteem statistics, suggests that girls who are taught the dynamics of racism at home internalize strategies that prevented them from personalizing behavioral assaults that could injure their self-esteem (Marilyn Webb, 1992). Self-esteem is internally centered; thus the affirmation of our young girls must be based not on external measures of attractiveness and appeal to men, but attached to a healthy internal sense of self, grounded in their own aspirations and accomplishments.

Self-Recovery

Recovery after a defeat, failure or setback can provide impetus for unparalleled success if the individual is able to see opportunity in a previously negative situation or outcome. Many people permit a negative circumstance or experience to defeat their purpose, derail their plans, and circumvent their goals. Self-recovery is a bouncing-back process that begins with an assessment of how and why you failed. You must remember that failure can breathe success and success is exploitation of your failure(s). When you get into such absolutistic thinking as "I will always fail," "I will never succeed," you have caged or entombed yourselves in the permanence of failure. You have psychologically defined yourselves as incompetent, uneducable, and unrehabilitable. You might as well roll over and permanently hibernate. The negative and positive are part of life just as love and hate, good and bad, competent and incompetent, and success and failure. How you turn the negative into a positive is a learnable skill.

Self-Renewal

A major reason why adults are inclined to limit their learning springs from their unwillingness to take risks. Learning is a risky phenomenon that is fraught with failure. Adults detest failure. In infancy, youngsters learn at an accelerated rate that rapidly declines as they get older. They experience multiple failures, but tolerate little discouragement or defeat. By puberty and late adolescence, the motivation of these young people to take risks greatly diminishes. Parents' insistence that their children learn, and their punishment of failure engender fear, and cause the inner drive of these youths to evaporate, thus making the goal of success appear "perilous" to young people. By adulthood, many of these individuals have developed a dislike for risk-taking, and carry the baggage of things they are unwilling to ever try again because of the "perils" of failure, parental condemnation and punishment, or the mediocre performance their self-esteem refuses to accept.

Often, however, these low risk-takers become involved with spouses, lovers, bosses, or business partners who do not understand or recognize that their low-risk taking history is related to failure, so they push, cajole, insult, threaten, redicule, and abuse these reluctant risk-takers (Gardner, 1964).

The ability to take risks, and our capacity to tolerate failure were present in all of us as infants. Self-renewal is the process of regaining the ability to take risks and the capacity to bounce back. Risk-taking, a vital part of mature adult behavior, would not magically reappear. It requires an expenditure of energy, effort, and hard work as denoted by the prefix "self" as in self-renewal. No one can do this for you; you have to do it for yourself. Others can empathize and assist, but it is a self-exploratory process. Thus self-renewal is finding the comfortability and creativity in taking risks and learning

from failure to increase your accomplishments and gain
social upliftment and success. Self-discovery is the
exploratory process that identifies the psychological injury
and behavioral wounds that are gapingly deep, but which
must be identified before any development of self-esteem can
occur.

The level or extent of one's injury varies across and within
gender and ethnoculturally-different groups. Some women
and culturally different individuals, who have been down-
trodden for decades and relegated to a caste of inferior
treatment, and fragmented family systems are likelier than
most to have lower levels of self-esteem. Boys, who are generally socialized to believe they are capable, smart, competent,
and infallible, seem to sustain only superficial wounds to
their self-esteem. Consequently, they need less self-esteem
boosting if any at all. Girls, however, who were taught to limit
their aspirations and expectations may have a more serious
problem. They are viewed as weaker, less cerebral, incapable,
not good enough, cannot measure up, told they are wall
flowers, or ornaments to adorn the masculine ego, and that
their place is a subservient one. Understandably, many may
have deeper wounds and scars, and be in need of greater
doses of self-image and self-esteem rehabilitation.

Chapter Eleven

Breaking Permanently with the Past

> Sustained change and relapse prevention are life-
> long processes a motivated survivor undertakes
> unconditionally.
>
> V. Michael McKenzie, Ph.D.

Ambition and Stagnation

For most people ambition is a positive force, fighting the
fires of their passions and inspiring them to create and
achieve. An enormous commitment of time and energy is
required to satisfy ambition. The payoff is responsibility,
challenge, and advancement (Adele Scheele, 1992).

Ambition or the desire to want and strive for more in life is a
relatively new phenomenon for most women, who have been
socialized to repress their goals and dreams. This
unfortunate conditioning of women to suffocate their aspirations has worked to the advantage of men. Women have often
sacrificed their youth, autonomy, and dreams, and postponed
developing themselves, friendships, social networks, education, career, and extra curricula goals. Society has condi-
tioned women to be passive, accommodating, cheerful, nice,
forgiving, and sacrificial. By sublimating their wants and
denying their dreams, women have been able to put the needs

and feelings of men, children, and others ahead of their own. As a result, they have generally been unassertive, docile, laissez-faire, unambitious, shy, superficial, timid, reluctant, confused, willing to take the back seat to avoid conflict, and unmotivated to pursue their modest or lofty dreams. They have learned to be low-profiled, quiet, unobtrusive, and a faithful companion, who seldom if ever complains. This is changing ever too slowly.

To fulfill your dreams and empower yourself, a woman must be willing to be ambitious, have realistic goals and dreams, travel first class, assertively stand up for her beliefs as elegantly or as boisterously as she chooses. She must reject the status quo, live her dreams and desires, develop her drive and overcome the fear, anxiety, frustration and depression of unrealized dreams and unfulfilled needs. Wage and win the internal battles of negative thoughts, feelings, and per- ceptions that impede your desire to be all you can be. Do not be limited by your femaleness and imprisoned by your past. Defy your female gender-role expectations and limitations. Inertia is a hangman's noose—it will suffocate your ambitions and eventually strangle you. Acknowledge your fear, but persevere because it is the only way to defeat fear. Women who attempt to actualize their ambitions will be faced with obstacles most men are not likely to encounter (criticism, discouragement, envy, broken friendships, gender-biased behaviors and institutions). Dr. Adele Scheele points out:

> Some people undoubtedly will be threatened by her success. They may not like her as much as they did before. They may even seek revenge by sabotaging her efforts to perform well in her new job. When women step out of the traditional role of serving others and into the role of leader, they are sometimes punished. They are labeled bitches or, worse, rumored to be sleeping their way to the top.

The road to success is not always smooth. There is an ugly side to ambition. "Blind ambition" can hurt those who are so driven by a need for unbridled power, status, fame, and money that they resort to deceit, cheating, illegality, lying, game-playing, and manipulation to achieve their goals. The ugly side of ambition, most evident in the 1980's decade of greed, may result more from a dysfunctional personality constellation than the purely ambitious drive.

Some people are like retiring thorough bred race horses. They are highly motivated during the warm-up exercises, accomplish the short-range goal of starting the race, but burn out quickly and fade into extinction before completing the race. Here are six indicators that you may be losing your ambition and drive:

- You admire ambitious people and those who seek a better life, yet, you associate with individuals who are unambitious, lazy, and unmotivated.

- You are inspired by those who are progressive and career-oriented, but you seldom follow through on your own dreams, creativity, and constructive ideas.

- You are low on risk-taking behaviors but big on externalizing and blaming circumstance for your malaise and inaction.

- You have the talent and can find the resources to become a success, but live in a fantasy world of indecision and inaction.

- You admire or are envious of the success of others, but are fearful and depressed about seeking your own achievements.

- You are constantly pushing a spouse, child, friend, or relative to aspire and achieve, but your goals are frozen or nonexistent.

Decision-Making and Failure

As women tenaciously grasp their traditionally female roles and patterns of behavior, they will continue to assume that they do not know much, consequently, they cannot make important decisions. Thus, they avoid the decision-making process. This behavior reinforces their fear, and robs them of the self-confidence building experiences inherent in taking risks. It forces them into avoidance behaviors hence inaction. If a woman makes a sound decision, it is often attributed to luck or someone else gets the credit. Men generally exude self-confidence and an air of superiority in their decision-making behavior even if, in their enthusiasm to be decisive, mistakes are made. Experience in the workplace has demonstrated that a poor decision may evoke less punitive action than indecision. If one's decision is grounded in logic, reason, and the best information available, then the ensuing results should irrefutably be the best that was humanly attainable. This is often unacceptable to many women. Some frightened individuals complain, and vacillate under the most ideal decision-making circumstances thus avoiding the responsibility of making a decision. Others may make a decision under the best available circumstances, yet engage in self-condemnation, feel like a failure, withdraw, and resort to more negative evaluation of their behavior.

Decision-making, like so many other activities, has an emotional as well as a behavioral component. If the emotional side (fear, anxiety, anger, hurt) dominates you, the whole decision-making process may be crippled or poorly executed. High levels of emotionality can be harmful to just about any process. Similarly, if the emotions are kept to a manageable or moderate level, but the behaviors (indecision, lack of preparation, poor skill-level, lack of impulse control, premature action) are absent or inappropriate, the decision-making can be less than optimum. For a woman to overcome the fear of decision-making, she needs to make an objective evaluation of where she is emotionally and behaviorally. We understand the importance of decision-making in relationships and career choices, and the critical role emotions and behavior play. Should I leave or should I stay in an abusive relationship? Should I marry the man or woman who treats me disrespectfully, but whom I love? Should I apply for that senior position that entails more responsibility, longer work hours, a substantial salary increase, but the eventual loss of close friends by becoming the boss? Decision making is complex. It involves identifying and evaluating the risk factors, weighing the possible gains versus the potential losses for each option available, and the course of action one wants to exercise. Most decision-making behavior involves taking action with predictable or uncertain outcome. One can reduce uncertainty by understanding and managing the emotions that impede decision-making, and develop the behaviors and skills that help effective decision-making.

John W. Gardner (1964) observed:

> We pay a heavy price for our fear of failure. It is a powerful obstacle to growth. It assures the progressive narrowing of the personality and prevents exploration and experimentation. There is no learning without some difficulty and fumbling. If you want to keep on learning, you must keep on risking failure all your life.

Failure is the feedback component, and a critical part of the learning process. It informs us that we have scored in the deficit or minus column of the learning curve. When we experience failure, however, many of us often become distraught, angry, or so resentful that we are unable to benefit from the feedback failure provides. A mature and positive evaluation of failure should not produce feelings or behavior beyond annoyance, inconvenience, displeasure or disappointment. For some people failure provides motivation and excitement about trying again, and a willingness to learn from that experience. The negative evaluation of failure is likely to precipitate anger, resentment, humiliation, embarrassment, withdrawal, isolation, or refusal to try again. Some individuals experience failure at such a personal-emotional level that they consider themselves to be a failure with little or no self-worth. At a deeper emotional level, fear of failure and failure itself, decision-making, risk-taking, competition and ambition are part of a complex set of phenomena related to self-confidence, self-image, self-esteem, assertiveness, a positive mental attitude, and healthy self-acceptance.

Self-Acceptance

Self-acceptance includes your physical, behavioral and psychological makeup—physical appearance, speech and behavioral patterns, character, attributes, strengths and weaknesses, emotionality and temperament. Are you able to tolerate and accept your feelings when you are disappointed, frustrated, depressed, fearful or angry without engaging in self-destructive behavior? Can you experience joy, laughter, praise, love when things are going well in your life? An ability to experience your feelings without denying (repressing and avoiding) them is the crux of self-acceptance. How do you talk about yourself and your experiences of life? Do you belittle, condemn or otherwise put yourself down? Are your negative thoughts and self-evaluations an every-day occurrence? Do they lodge in your unconscious and wreak havoc on your personality? If you believe and expect that you are not deserving of the best and finer things in life, the self-fulfilling prophecy kicks in and you get exactly what you expect? In other words, you behave according to your negative belief system and expectations, and the results are correspondingly negative?

As you engage in correcting the damage to your self-esteem, you may begin with converting your negative thoughts, negative internal dialogue or self-talk, and negative self-evaluations to their opposite polarity. You change the negative thoughts, feelings, and behavior to positive thoughts, feelings, and behavior.

A Self-Acceptance Exercise

This exercise should not be done by those individuals who have a psychiatric diagnosis, or others who are often devas-tated by negative comments or feedback (Towers, 1991). Those with an anorexic and/or bulimic diagnosis are cautioned not to do this exercise under any circumstance. Individuals who are in counseling may check with their counselor before proceeding.

Materials Required:

1. A full length mirror in your bedroom or some other private place
2. An emotionally honest and trusted spouse, friend, (girlfriend or boyfriend)
3. A tape recorder or notebook and pencil
4. Time 25 to 35 minutes

Sessions

1. This exercise requires courage. Clad in a close-fitting swim suit, swim trunks, or preferably your birthday suit (in the nude), stand before the full-size mirror, and observe your body fully and completely. For ten to fourteen minutes examine your torso, gut, stomach, arms, toes, right and left sides of your body, face, hair, lips, thighs, breasts, chin, eyes, buttocks, teeth, complexion, stretch marks, and neck including all

the sags and bulges that are evident. Focus on and record your thoughts and feelings mentally first, then on the tape recorder, or in your notebook. Block out all distractions as best you can, and concentrate on how your body looks in the full-length mirror. Note carefully what you see and how you feel about what you see. Stay in the present here-and-now. Do not focus on and consider what you hope your appearance will be the next day or some future date, or what you looked like before the exercise (maybe when you were slim). Stay with what presents itself to you in the mirror.

2. After you have fully observed your body from head to toe, left to right, and completely absorbed the experience, you should begin to record your observations, thoughts, feelings, and behavior. Some individuals prefer to make these recordings during the observation period; that is acceptable. As was indicated earlier, a notebook or tape recorder can be used.

3. Repeat the entire exercise except this time your friend or spouse will make the observations and record his or her thoughts, feelings, and direct observations either on the tape recorder or in a notebook. This second observation should occur the same day or within a day or two.

4. Equipped with your recorded data, and that of your friend or spouse, retire to a private and quiet place. Take as much time as you desire to review and digest both sets of data. As a guide, you can focus on the following: What imperfections did you see? Did you identify bulges, overweight, stretch marks, saggy breasts, cuts and bruises, evidence of poor nutrition, too many chemicals in your hair, poor dental care, lack of exercise, bloated stomach, enlarged navel, enlarged nose, or a totally unattractive body? What

else did you not like about your body? What negative thoughts did you have of your general appearance? What feelings did you get in contact with? Were you filled with a sense of pride, joy, and happiness as you observed your body, or were you upset, critical, sad and displeased? After you have been fully saturated with your negative reactions turn your attention to the positive reactions you had, and with what attributes were these associated? What did you like about your body? Some individuals discover that they detest and criticize this strange person they see in the mirror, and with whom they have been living for whatever time. Many are pleased and impressed, whereas, others reported having mixed feelings. What was your overall reaction to the you reflected in the mirror?

5. Review the comments of your spouse or friend in a comparative fashion. How does your spouse or friend's profile compare to yours? Are the two sets of comments identical? If not, how would you roughly evaluate their similarity in percentage (90, 70, 50, 25, or less than 15 percent similar)? Was the other observer or evaluator honest, kind, insulting, humorous, empathic? Have you heard similar comments from this person or others before? How does it make you feel to know others see you this way, and what happens in your mind when such comments are made?

6. What negative thoughts or memories did this exercise evoke?

   What were your resistances to doing this exercise?

   What self-doubts did you get in touch with during and after this exercise?

   What parts of yourself were you most ashamed of, and how did you plan to conceal them?

   How have you concealed them before?

Devise a list of words that precisely define the person you saw in the mirror—the way you felt, the thoughts you had. To help you accomplish this the following list is provided.

1.	Angry	Depressed	Ecstatic
2.	Forgiving	Challenged	Fearful
3.	Sad	Empowered	Bored
4.	Terminal	Self-aware	Diminished
5.	Manipulated	Happy	Fortunate
6.	Responsible	Different	Unique
7.	Unfortunate	Worried	Uncertain
8.	Deprived	Reflective	Tense
9.	Impulsive	Unloved	Bulgy
10.	Energized	Impoverished	Disgusted
11.	Esteemed	Passive	Obese
12.	Burnout	Elated	Accusatory
13.	Blaming	Guilt	Change
14.	Displacement	Regret	Help
15.	Stop	Try harder	Give up
16.	Love	Hate	Commitment
17.	Ugly	Action	Energy
18.	Worried	Incentive	Foolish
19.	Motivation	Parents	Spouse
20.	Serious	Unrealistic	Tense
21.	Foolish	Careless	Impulsive
22.	Isolated	Lonely	Alone
23.	Cover-up	Conceal	Hide
24.	Strange	Diet	Exercise
25.	Gregarious	Solitude	Different
26.	New	Self-image	Self-confidence
27.	Hideous	Indifferent	Uncaring

7. This is the most difficult part and the real essence of the exercise. Can you or were you able to love, appreciate, like, admire, and accept yourself exactly as you were revealed to be in the mirror exercise? Rate your level of self-acceptance by percentage before and after the exercise—100, 75, 50, 25, or less than 15 percent.

Individuals with poor self-esteem generally have a negative self-image as well. Your self-image does not come from the mirror or another person's evaluation of you in your adult years. Self-image comes from within. As Mark Towers (1991) noted:

Lack of self-esteem is like being psychologically anorexic. No matter how thin you are, you look in the mirror and see the same overweight/unacceptable person. . . . A poor self-image is like looking in a cloudy mirror that always reflects back the same unacceptable person to us, no matter how many external changes we make.

If you hated and despised what you saw in the mirror your self-image may be extremely negative. If you can love and accept yourself unconditionally then your self-image is in the positive zone. Unconditional self-acceptance and self-love equal self-image. Self-acceptance and love are different from complacency or a desire for change and improvement. Self-image, and, therefore, self-esteem are loving and valuing yourself now, today, in the here-and-now; whereas, change or improvement is a future state. If you value and love yourself as revealed in the mirror, but desire change and improvement in the future, your self-esteem and self-image are within normal limits. If, however, you indicate that you will love and value yourself (which may never occur) after losing thirty pounds, when you secure the ideal job, after you join the millionaire women's club, or when you are able to buy a foreign-made sports car, then this external and conditional state is testimony of poor self-esteem and a negative self-image. If during this exercise, you discover aspects of yourself you would like to change, the section on goal-setting, in this chapter, will be helpful.

Your self-image, which is directly related to your self-esteem, can be negatively affected when you are manipulated by people and events over which you have very little or no control. Your self-image is affected when you are demeaned or subjugated in a relationship, victimized by gender-biased behavior or your occupational role is demeaning. If you are an exploiter or manipulator of other human beings, you may as well be damaging your self-image and self-esteem. More specifically, not being able to experience yourself as an involved and valued member of your family or work group, wherein, your contributions to problem-solving and cohesive-ness are recognized can be a major source of lowered self-esteem. A healthy level of self-esteem and a good self-image can withstand any assault on your psyche.

Self-Recognition

Many women, including First Lady Hillary Rodham Clinton, have been severely criticized for retaining and using their maiden or family name. Apart from its political state-ments, a married woman's retention of her maiden name is a positive self-affirmation. This risk-taking behavior is indica-tive of good self-esteem and a healthy self-image. The self-recognition is healthy and positive, and an adaptive reversal of putting other peoples' needs (names) before her own. Use of one's maiden name is the self-acceptance of a woman's estab-lished identity many insecure men and some women have been critical of. Self-recognition is the emotional and behav-ioral comfortability in relishing your accomplishments privately as well as publicly. Self-recognition rejects the expectation that women should be submissive, nice, and sublimate their needs. Self-recognition is the celebrating of one's achievements or gains however modest. It is the self-generated positive reinforcement for any accomplishment (returning to school or work, ending an abusive relationship, reporting sexual harassment, completing a course in carpentry or assertive behavior, starting your own business, becoming provost of a major university, winning political office). Self-recognition is saying no without feeling guilty, and not having to compromise your values, engage in offensive behavior, or measure up to someone else's unrealistic code of behavior. Self-recognition entails, according to the *Webster's Dictionary*, "recognition of one's self." Self-recognition is one of the important elements in self-esteem.

Self-Praise

The Academy Award nominations and the award itself, the Grammy or Tony, the Pulitzer or Nobel Peace Prizes are all accolades or credits given to individuals or groups for their achievement. Self-praise is giving yourself credit for what you have achieved. As Mark Towers observed, "When people ask, 'What do you do?' Do you feel apologetic and defensive, murmuring, 'Oh I'm just a secretary/accountant/house-wife/salesman?' " The standards by which we judge success are biased, and many of us internalize these biased standards by which we evaluate ourselves and others; thus, non-professional or non-compensatory work is seldom given high credit. Raising a child in today's troubled times, managing a family's budget against inflation, engaging in voluntary community work, or being a single working parent are examples of complex activities for which one deserves and should be given credit. When individuals see themselves as a failure, it is generally related to their perceptions, expectations, values, belief system, and negative evaluations of themselves and what they do occupationally. To trivialize, minimize, or negate what you legitimately do for a living is a symptom of poor self-esteem.

Breaking with the Past

Human beings behave the only way they know how, so they keep their earlier dysfunctional experiences alive through their thoughts, feelings, and behavior. The human mind is like a videotape, it records life's events and experiences in vivid color and replays them constantly at will. The negative experiences stored in our unconscious can be worked through irrespective of how deep our psychological wounds and scars are. Regardless of how severe you have been wounded by your parents, caregivers, or other people, and what counterproductive decisions you made in your life, it is unhealthy to hold on to pain, anger, resentment, negative emotions, and dysfunctional behaviors. To allow yourself to remain trapped in a negative emotional and behavioral pattern is a psychological death sentence. You can commute your death sentence by letting go of the past and its baggage of fear, indecision, passivity, low risk-taking, and the other maladaptive patterns or negativity. "Self-esteem requires and entails cognitive self-assertiveness, which is expressed through the policy of thinking, of judging, and of governing action accordingly" (Branden, 1969). Human beings need to find ways of increasing their self-esteem that directly and positively affect their self-confidence, self-image, self-actualization, and overall psychological health.

When our self-esteem has bottomed out and our energy is low, taking action and setting goals do not receive our priority. Clearly, without goals one can drift aimlessly in a sea of inaction, carried by the waves of resentment and unresolved conflict, baked by the hot sun of anger and unforgiveness, relieved occasionally by a thick cloud of denial, but always swept deeper and deeper into a psychological morass by the incompassionate winds of despair and intransigence.

Goal-Setting

> Goal-setting is not a term one hears very often within the Latino culture. I first heard it while working at the university and the concept baffled me because the words themselves had no meaning for me. When colleagues at the university asked me what my goals were, I would naïvely respond, "I really don't have any." My colleagues looked at me as if to say, "Look, you dummy, everybody has goals!" After all, I was twenty-eight-years old (Flores, 1990).

Let us briefly revisit the discussion of indecision to emphasize the point that the toughest part of getting your needs met in life is deciding what it is that you want. Goal-setting is an effective motivational method for launching yourself on a path to results-oriented action. Critical-incidents studies have demonstrated that goal setting can be a principal determinant of increased productivity in human beings resulting in an enhanced willingness to assume future challenges. In their book titled, *Goal Setting: A Motivational Technique That Works* (1984), Edwin Locke and Gary Latham cited critical studies' findings that indicated goal-setting helps to clarify expectations, build self-confidence, and enhance pride in achievement. Additionally, goal-setting relieves boredom, generates feelings of competence, and increases spontaneous competition. When we set goals, our performance and the task itself bring us more satisfaction in job performance. When goals are properly designed and implemented, goal-setting increases self-esteem, self-confidence, and self-image. The principle to be emphasized here is specific goals and direct action are more reliably productive and life enhancing than vague, global, or general and non-specific goals. When goal-setting is done with specificity and follow-through behaviors are based on internal commitment, you are challenged to overcome:

- Indecision and behavioral stagnation
- Self-imposed and societal limitations
- Failure and the fear of failure
- The lack of self-acceptance and self-confidence
- Negative self-talk, negative put-downs, and negative self-appraisal

Goal-setting allows you to design and set increasingly difficult and creative goals that build on your prior achievements. As you become deeply immersed in the process of goal-setting and goal realization, you achieve higher levels of awareness that permits greater self-discovery. Greater self-discovery leads to a recognition of hidden talents and potentials that, when claimed and nurtured, can lead to self-acceptance, self-fulfillment, self-recognition, and self-recovery.

As was previously mentioned, greater self-esteem, self confidence and a healthier self-image are all connected. Goal-setting has been used with exceedingly great success in multi-million dollar organizations for over seventy years. However, behavioral scientists have only in the last two decades subjected goal-setting to the rigorous and systematic experimental examination required. Apart from the critical-studies' findings mentioned, laboratory studies that were replicated in the organizational settings produced the same positive results. Thus, individuals who pursue challenging and specific goals gain more than those who settle for vague and global goals such as "I will do my best," or "I will change my life." One cautionary note is appropriate here. Goal-setting and goal realization are not a panacea for all our ills and dysfunctions. Achieving a goal will not make your life a perfect success story. For instance, if you have poor self-esteem, a negative self-image, fear of failure, and a history of psychological abuse, but manage to achieve your goal of a high-paying, high-profile job—do you think this career path will magically obliterate your psychological and behavioral problems? This is not likely.

Although goal realization may represent a major milestone in your life, and bring you many important financial and psychological rewards, the unresolved under-lying issues will continue to be problematic in your life. Getting a prized job, finding the ideal lover or spouse, having a baby, divorcing the stereotypically cantankerous wife or neglectful husband, or buying an expensive toy are all defensive maneuvers unconsciously aimed at denying, avoiding, or postponing the resolution of psychologically-based personal problems.

What may be helpful is to have multiple goals. As we have just discussed, an individual may be in a career rut while simultaneously experiencing personal-emotional and psychological-behavioral problems. Individuals should not restrict or compartmentalize their goals to just one or two areas of their life, but examine the entire spectrum. By designing goals in multiple life areas, you demonstrate to yourself that you are not neglecting painful aspects of your life. Also, as you begin to realize your goals, your achievement occurs in a more balanced or holistic manner. So, for instance, if you had set a career and psychological goal, the simultaneous achievement of these goals would bring greater personal satisfaction to your life. Some of the major categories for designing and implementing goals include, but are not limited to:

- Occupational, career or work
- Education and training
- Psychological remediation and development
- Interpersonal relationship goals
- Self-actualization and creative self-expression
- Lifestyle changes
- Recreation and leisure
- Spiritual or religious goals

Some individuals believe they have the capacity to pursue only one goal at a time. Rather than be judgmental, let us draw on our knowledge of fear of failure, indecision, poor self-image, low risk-taking and so on to demonstrate empathic understanding for those whose perceptions and behaviors are self-limiting. Multiple goal-setting and the simultaneous accomplishment of several goals are doable. The prioritizing of goals involves a ranking of your goals by order of significance or immediacy. You may desire to work on your short-term goals because they can be accomplished in a fairly easier manner. The results of your short-range goals may be required as a prerequisite for work to begin on a long-range goal(s). For instance, your long-range goals to be accomplished in five years may involve buying a house or new car. Your short-range goals may be to accelerate completion of your college degree (take an extra course at night or on weekends, explore credits for work-related experiences), postpone your wedding until after you have acquired your home, marry your boyfriend or girlfriend so the double-team efforts can yield more financially. You can use this long-term goal as a good reason to get a higher paying job, or take the part-time work you were so indecisive about. These short-term goals are examples of how you can facilitate the realization of a long-range goal.

A case with which I have worked in private practice involved a client's pursuit of counseling to alleviate panic attacks, which was her short-term goal. The panic attacks increased her absenteeism from work, reduced her earning capability, and interfered with her long-range goal of moving to an affluent suburban neighborhood. Mark Towers (1991) stated it very well when he wrote:

> Goal-setting is a form of starting over, but it requires a kind of spring cleaning before you begin. It's called "clearing." You need to clear out psychological blocks that are holding you back from attaining your goals.

These psychological blocks as we have discussed earlier are related to negative childhood and other experiences that resulted in the repressed emotions of anger, fear, and guilt, and the behavioral barriers of indecision, procrastination, negative self-talk, and a host of others. Nothing keeps us more psychologically and behaviorally trapped and imprisoned than the pent-up feelings and unresolved emotions of anger, guilt, and fear, and the accompanying resentment and desire to seek revenge.

Goal-setting is not a difficult task. Although it is not within the scope of this book to present in detail the goal-setting methodology, enough information is being given to assist individuals who seek psychological well being, social upliftment, advancement and success in life. A prominent personality characteristic of individuals who are successful is a well-organized sense of purpose and direction. This sense of purpose is seen in the clarity and specificity of their goals.

Resilience is another behavioral characteristic of the successful individual. To the resilient person, failure to attain a goal offers an opportunity to redefine and re-prioritize goals instead of generating and harboring feelings of doom and despair.

Resilience and flexibility emerge as this person explores and creates alternative ways to satisfy similar ends. His or her goals are not so contradictory as to generate a "damned if I do, and damned if I don't" life situation. In short, the successful individual experiences a high degree of Goal Confidence (Pamela Cuming, 1981).

There are at least seven key steps in goal-setting when optimum results are the objective (Locke and Latham, 1984). They include:

- Itemize in specific terms the general objective or task to be accomplished.
- Define the goal and specify how the performance will be measured.
- Specify targets or standards to be achieved.
- Specify the time involved.
- Prioritize goals.
- Rate goals as to level of significance and difficulty.
- Determine additional requirements—is attainment of the goal dependent on outside help such as the efforts of or resources from others?

It is important to recognize that goal achievement can be hampered by the following:

- Unrealistic and difficult or overly-complex goals.
- Undefined, non-specific, and non-measurable goals.
- Goals lacking your full ownership because they were designed by others and don't reflect your desires.
- Overly rigid and inflexible about your defined goals.
- Withdrawal instead of re-organization and re-prioritization when goal-attainment fails. Goal-setting must be treated as a flexible process in which modification and refinement constantly take place.

- Skill deficiency—the individual may lack the ability and/or behavior required to achieve a goal. For example, an indecisive person may have poor decision-making skills; a person wanting to get married and have a family may not know how to meet a prospective spouse; a nervous entertainer may not know how to sufficiently reduce his or her anxiety for optimum performance.

- Knowledge deficiency—the individual may lack the information required for achieving a goal. For instance, a woman desiring to be a business entrepreneur may not be aware of government small business loans or women set asides. An obese person wishing to lose weight on a do-it-yourself diet may not know the caloric intake of certain foods.

- Lack of risk-taking skills—the person may have the knowledge and skills, but is psychologically blocked from taking action to realize his or her goals. The man or woman desiring a spouse may be paralyzed from taking action by the fear of rejection. The entrepreneur knows how to create a business enterprise but fears failure.

The Action Plan

An action plan is in essence a written blue print; it delineates in descriptive form the ways and means of accomplishing your goals. It specifies what action will be taken, when, how, where and why. The action plan entails the means and ends including the cost in time, money and effort. The plan focuses on the most immediate decisions and tasks for accomplishing the short-range goals, and the most important long-term goals and their strategies. Since the action plan is a written guide it has the following advantages. Some of those identified by Carroll and Tosi (1973) include:

- Action plans force us to make a commitment in writing as a tangible first step
- Action plans facilitate the search for efficient and effective techniques for attaining your goals
- They reflect the reality of whether or not the stated goals are achievable
- They highlight time, cost, and other resources required for goal attainment
- They provide the opportunity to re-examine your goals and determine if the help of others is required for the goals to be accomplished
- Action plans help to identify snags and obstacles that block goal attainment

Finally, a goal can be defined as the behavioral outcome the individual strives for. An effectively stated outcome goal has within it the targeted behavior to be changed. So the behavioral outcome, and outcome goal can be one and the same. For example, an individual may target the reduction of negative self-evaluation as the behavioral outcome goal, whereas, another person may choose as his or her behavioral outcome more assertive responses in the workplace and at home. In both cases, the reduction of negative self-appraisal and more assertive responses are both the behavior to be modified and the identified goal to be achieved. Besides behavioral outcome goals, one has to specify the conditions under which his or her behavioral changes will occur. You must be clear about the settings where behavioral changes will occur because some settings can promote or hinder successful change or goal attainment. If an obese individual is striving to fulfill the primary or short-range goal of working to defray college expenses, and the long-range goal of losing seventy-five pounds to enhance health and employment opportunities, placing him or her in a bakery or restaurant setting would be tantamount to failure. Another important factor in outcome goals is the realistic and appropriate level of behavioral change you have targeted in your goals. Someone choosing to lose seventy-five pounds in one month or reduce daily caloric intake from 7,000 to 1,300 may be dangerously unrealistic and failure-bound. You may not realize it, but every time you set and modify your goals you gain a closer approximation to your ultimate result.

From Victim to Survivor

The road from victim to survivor has an uncertain destination when the battered woman procrastinates, vacillates, and sabotages her recovery process. Psychological healing is a process fraught with pain and emotional discomfort. If a victim is tenacious, she engages in the struggle, and grapples with the pain inherent in change. The rewards of change blossom slowly, but with a certainty that matches the survivor's determination.

References

Argyris, C. *Increasing Leadership Effectiveness*. New York: Wiley, 1976.

Arias, I., Samios, M., and O'Leary, K. D. "Prevalence and Correlates of Physical Aggression During Courtship." *Journal of Interpersonal Violence*, 1987, 2:82-90.

Barnlund, D. C. "Communicative Styles in Two Cultures: Japan and the United States." *Organization of Behavior in Face-To-Face Interaction*. Edited by A. Kendon, R. M. Harris and M. R. Key. The Hague: Mouton, 1975.

Bass, E., and Davis, L. *Beginning to Heal: A First Book for Survivors of Child Sexual Abuse*. New York: Harper Collins Publishers, Inc., 1993.

Blocher, D. H. *Developmental Counseling*. New York: John Wiley and Sons, 1974.

Bolton, R. G., Reich, J. W., and Guiterres, S. E. "Delinquency Patterns in Maltreated Children and Siblings." *Victimology*, 1977, 2:349-357.

Bowker, L. H., Arbitell, M., and McFerron, J. R. "On the Relationship between Wife Beating and Child Abuse." *Feminist Perspectives on Wife Abuse*. Edited by K. Yllo and M. Bogard. Newbury Park, CA: Sage, 1988, 162.

Bradshaw, J. *The Family: A Revolutionary Way of Self-Discovery*. Deerfield Beach, FL: Health Communications, Inc., 1993.

Bradshaw, J. *Healing the Shame That Binds You*. Deerfield Beach, FL: Health Communications, Inc., 1988.

Branden, N. "Woody Allen: Loss of a Hero." *New Woman*, November, 1992, pp. 42-43.

————. *The Psychology of Self-Esteem*. New York: Bantam Books, 1969.

Broome, B. J. "Facilitating Attitudes and Message Characteristics in the Expression of Differences in Intercultural Encounters." *International Journal of Intercultural Relations*, 1981, 5, 215-237.

Browne, A. *When Battered Women Kill*. New York: Free Press, 1987.

Carlson, B. E. "Dating Violence: A Research Review and Comparison with Spouse Abuse." *Social Casework*, 1987, 68:16-23.

Carroll, S. J. and Tosi, H. L. *Management by Objectives*. New York: Macmillan, 1973, 81-82.

Chodorow, N. "Family Structure and Feminine Personality." *Women, Culture and Society*. Edited by M. Z. Rosaldo and L. Lamphere. Stanford: Stanford University Press, 1974.

Colorado Domestic Violence Coalition. *Domestic Violence for Health Care Providers*. 3rd ed., 1991.

————. *Colorado Standards for Intervention with Court Ordered Domestic Violence Perpetrators*. Denver, CO. 1991.

Cuming, P. *The Power Handbook: A Strategic Guide to Organizational and Personal Effectiveness*. Boston, MA: CBI Publishing Co., Inc., 1981.

Darling, L. "Finally, We Can Deal with Authority Figures." *Self*, September, 1990, p. 217.

Davis, R. "Abuse Knows No Social Boundaries." *USA Today*, June 20, 1994, p. 3A.

Diagnostic and Statistical Manual of Mental Disorders. 3rd ed., revised. Washington, D.C.: American Psychiatric Association, 1987.

Dillard, J. M. *Multicultural Counseling: Toward Ethnic and Cultural Relevance in Human Encounters*. Chicago: Nelson-Hall Inc., 1983.

"Domestic Violence Intervention Calls for More Treating Injuries." *JAMA: The Journal of the American Medical Association*, 1990, 264, (8), 939.

Domestic Violence: A Community Crisis Waiting for an Effective Response. Seattle Domestic Violence Intervention, 1989.

Duluth Domestic Abuse Intervention Project. *DAIP: The Domestic Abuse Intervention Project*. Duluth, MN. 1986.

Gutmann, D. "The Cross-Cultural Perspective: Notes Toward a Comparative Psychology of Aging." *Handbook of the Psychology of Aging.* Edited by J. E. Birren and K. Warner Schaie. New York: Van Nostrand, 1977.

Hammond, W. R. and Yung, B. R. *Dealing With Anger: Giving it, Taking it, Working it out.* Champaign, IL: Research Press, 1991.

Harlow, C. W. "Female Victims of Violent Crime (NCJ-126826)." Rockville, MD: U.S. Department of Justice, 1991.

Harris, J. G. "A Science of the South Pacific: An Analysis of the Character Structure of the Peace Corp Volunteer." *American Psychologist,* 1973, 28, 232-247.

Hart, B. "Children of Domestic Violence: Risks and Remedies." *Protective Services Quarterly,* 1993.

————. *Accountability: Program Standard for Batterer Intervention Service.* Pennsylvania Coalition Against Domestic Violence (PCADV), 1992.

————. "Lesbian Battering: An Examination." *Aegis,* 1986, 41:19-28.

Heisler, C., Carter, J., and Lemon, N. "Domestic Violence: The Crucial Role of the Judge in Criminal Court Cases." *A National Model for Judicial Education.* Family Violence Prevention Fund, 1991, 94-95.

Hilts, P. J. "Six Percent of Women Report Beatings while Pregnant." *New York Times,* March, 1994.

Hoff, L. A. *Battered Women as Survivors.* New York: Routledge, 1990.

Hyde, J. S. "How Large Are Cognitive Gender Differences in Aggression? A Developmental Meta-Analysis." *Developmental Psychology,* 1984, 20, 722-736.

Ingrassia, M., and Beck, M. "Battered Women: Patterns of Abuse." *Newsweek,* July 4, 1994, pp. 26-33.

Jaffe, P., Wolfe, D., and Wilson, S. K. *Children of Battered Women.* Newbury Park, CA: Sage, 1990.

Johnson, M. P. "Violence Against Women in the American Family: Are There Two Forms?" Paper presented at Theory Construction and Research Methodology Workshop,

National Council on Family Relations, Baltimore, MD, 1993.

Kabat, S. "Simpson Case Shines Light on America's Dirty Secret." *St. Petersburg Times,* June, 1994, p. 10A.

Kalmuss, D. S. and Seltzer, J. A. "Continuity of Marital Behavior in Remarriage: The Case of Spouse Abuse." *Journal of Marriage and the Family,* 1986, 48:113-120.

Kendon, A. "Some Functions of Gaze Direction in Social Interaction." *Acta Psychologica,* 1967, 26, 22-63.

————. "Movement Coordination in Social Interaction: Some Samples Described." *Acta Psychologica,* 1970, 32, 100-125.

————. *Studies in Semiotics: Studies in the Behavior of Social Interaction.* Bloomington: Peter de Ridder Press, 1977.

Kleinjans, E. Opening Remarks at a Conference on World Communication held at the East West Center. Honolulu, Hawaii, 1972.

Koop, C. E. "Violence Against Women: A Global Problem." 1989.

Korda, M. *Male Chauvinism.* New York: Random House, 1972.

La France, M., and Mayo, C. "Racial Differences in Gaze Behavior during Conversation." *Journal of Personality and Social Psychology,* 1976, 33, 547-552.

Lakoff, R. T. *Talking Power.* New York: Basic Books, 1990.

LeMon, C. *Assertiveness: Get What You Want without Being Pushy.* Shawnee Mission, KS: National Press Pub., 1990.

Levison, F. B. "Coming Together in the Middle Years: A Longitudinal Study of Sex Role Convergence." The Double Standard of Aging: A Question of Sex Differences. Edited by B. F. Turner (Chair). Symposium conducted at the Annual Scientific Meeting of the Gerontological Society. New York, NY, October, 1976.

Locke, E. A., Latham, G. P. *Goal Setting: A Motivational Technique that Works.* Englewood Cliffs, NJ: Prentice Hall, Inc., 1984.

Maccoby, E. E., and Jacklin, C. N. *The Psychology of Sex Differences.* Stanford: Stanford University Press, 1974.

————. *Social Development: Psychological Growth and the Parent-Child Relationship.* New York: Harcourt, Brace Jovanovich, 1980.

Mahoney, M. R. "Legal Images of Battered Women: Redefining the Issue of Separation." *Michigan Law Review,* 1991, 90, 43-49.

Mayo, C. S., and Henley, N. M. *Gender and Nonverbal Behavior.* New York: Springer Verlag, 1981.

McDaniels, J. W. "The Effects of Leader Modeling Behavior and Didactic Communication Training on the Level of Open Expression in a Small Group Laboratory Training Experience." Paper presented in the Central State Speech Association Conference, April 4-6, 1974.

McFarlane, L. L. "Notes: Domestic Violence Victims v. Municipalities: Who Pays when the Police will not Respond?" *Case Western Reserve Law Review,* 1991, 929, 947, 104.

McFarlane, J. "Abuse during Pregnancy: A Cross-Cultural Study of Frequency and Severity of Injuries." *Public Health Nursing,* 1991.

McKenzie, V. M. "Managing Chronic Stress." *Ophthalmology Management,* 1988, 30-34.

————. "Ethnocultural Relevance in Clinical Treatment." Practice: *The Journal of Politics, Economics, Psychology, Sociology & Culture,* 1985, 3 (3), 101-113.

Millar. D. P., and Millar, F. E. *Messages and Myths: Understanding Interpersonal Communication.* New York: Alfred Publishing Co., Inc, 1976.

Miller, J. Baker. *Toward a New Psychology of Women.* Boston: Beacon Press, 1976.

Moir, A., and Jessel, D. *Brain Sex.* New York: Lyle Stuart, 1991.

Molloy, J. T. *Live for Success.* New York: Bantam Books, 1981.

Myers, G. D. *Psychology* (1st Ed.). New York: Worth Publishing, Inc., 1986.

National Aging Resource Center on Elder Abuse. Washington, D.C., 1990.

National Center on Women and Family Law. "How to Use the Immigration Act of 1990 to Help Battered Wives." *The Women's Advocate,* 1990, 13 (1), 3-6.

National Coalition Against Domestic Violence. *The 1994 National Directory of Domestic Violence Programs.* Denver, CO: NCADV, 1994.

―――. *The National Directory of Domestic Violence Programs.* Washington, D.C.: NCADV, 1991.

Nielsen, G. *Studies in Self-Confrontation.* Copenhagen: Munksgaard, 1964.

Paris, C., and Casey, B. *Project You: A Manual of Rational Assertiveness Training.* North Hollywood, CA: Wilshire Book Co., 1983.

Peck, M. Scott. *The Road Less Traveled: A New Psychology of Love, Traditional Values and Spiritual Growth.* New York: Simon and Schuster, 1978.

Pedersen, P. B., Lonner, W. J., and Draguns, J. G. (eds.). *Counseling Across Cultures.* Honolulu: University Press of Hawaii, 1976.

Richards, S. *Communication Skills.* Center City, MN: Hazelden, 1988.

Rogers, C. R. *On Becoming a Person: A Therapist's View of Psychotherapy.* Boston: Houghton Mifflin Co., 1961.

Roy, M. *Children in the Crossfire: Violence in the Home—How Does it Affect Our Children?* Deerfield Beach, FL: Health Communications, 1988.

Ruben, B. D. "Assessing Communication Competency for Intercultural Adaptation." *Group and Organization Studies,* 1976, 1, 335-354.

San Diego County Task Force on Domestic Violence. *Standards for the Treatment of Domestic Violence Perpetrators.* San Diego, CA: 1991.

Santa Clara County Domestic Violence Council and Board of Supervisors. *Standards for Batterers' Treatment Programs.* Santa Clara County, CA. 1994.

Saunders, D. G. "A Typology of Men Who Batter: Three Types Derived from Cluster Analysis." *American Journal of Orthopsychiatry,* 1992, 62(2), 264-275.

————. "Are there Different Types of Men Who Batter? An Empirical Study with Possible Implication for Treatment." *American Journal of Orthopsychiatry,* 1992, 62(2), 2-19.

————. "Profiling of Wife Assaulters: Preliminary Evidence for a Trimodal Analysis." *Violence and Victims,* 1988, 3:5-29.

————. "Issues in Conducting Treatment Research with Men Who Batter." *Coping with Family Violence: Research and Policy Perspectives.* Edited by G. Hotaling, D. Finkelhor, J. T. Kirlpatrich, and M. A. Straus. Newbury Park, CA: Sage, 1988, 145-156.

————. "Wife Abuse, Husband Abuse, or Mutual Combat? A Feminist Perspective on the Empirical Findings." *Feminist Perspectives on Wife Abuse.* Edited by K. Yllo and M. Bogard. Newbury Park, CA: Sage, 1988, 90-113.

Schaef, A. W. *Women's Reality: An Emerging Female System in a White Male Society.* Minneapolis, MN: Winston Press, 1985.

Schechter, S., and Gray, L. T. (1988). "A Framework for Understanding and Empowering Battered Women." *Abuse and Victimization Across the Life Span.* Edited by M. B. Straus. Baltimore, MD: The John Hopkins University Press, 1988, 240-252.

Scheele, A. "How Ambitious Are You?" *Working Woman,* March, 1992, pp. 30-32.

Schneider, E. "Legal Reform Efforts to Assist Battered Women: Past, Present and Future." Unpublished Report. Ford Foundation, 1990, pp. 21-22.

Seattle Domestic Violence Intervention. *Domestic Violence: A Community Crisis Waiting for an Effective Response.* 1989.

Senate Judiciary Committee Hearings. Section 741.28, Florida Statues, 1994.

Senate Judiciary Committee Hearings. Report on the Number of Shelters for Battered Women in the United States, 1990.

Skorneck, C. "Simpson Case Boosts Move against Domestic Violence." *The Tampa Tribune,* July 17, 1994, p. NW7.

Smith, P. K., and Danglish, L. "Sex Differences in Parent and Infant Behavior in the Home." *Child Development,* 1977, 8, 1250-1254.

Smolowe. J. "When Violence Hits Home." *Time,* July, 1994, pp. 19-25.

Stark, E., and Flitcraft, A. "Women and Children at Risk: A Feminist Perspective on Child Abuse." *International Journal of Health Services,* Vol. 18, No. I, 1988, 97-118.

————."Violence Among Inmates: An Epidemiological Review." *Handbook of Family Violence.* Edited by V. B. Van Hasselt, R. L. Morrison, A. S. Bellack and M. Hersen. New York: Plenum Press, 1988, 293-317.

————. "Medical Therapy as Repression: The Case of the Battered Woman." *Health and Medicine,* 1982, p. 31.

Stets, J. E. *Domestic Violence and Control.* New York: Springer Verlag, 1988.

Stevens, A. *The Roots of War.* New York: Paragon House, 1989.

Stoller, R. J. "A Contribution to the Study of Gender Identity." *International Journal of Psycho-Analysis,* 1964, 45:220-226.

Storr, A. *Human Aggression.* New York: Bantam Books, 1970.

Straus, M., and Gelles, R. *Physical Violence in American Families: Risk Factors and Adaptations to Violence in 8,145 Families.* New Brunswick, NJ: Transaction Publishers, 1990.

Straus, M. A., Gelles, R. J., and Steinmetz, S. K. *Behind Closed Doors: Violence in the American Family.* Garden City, NY: Doubleday, 1980.

Sue, D. W. *Counseling the Culturally Different.* New York: John Wiley and Sons, 1981.

————. "Evaluating Process Variables in Cross-Cultural Counseling/Therapy." *Cross-Cultural Counseling and Psychotherapy: Foundations, Evaluation and Cultural Considerations.* Edited by A. J. Marsella and P. Pedersen. Elmsford, New York: Pergamon, 1981.

Tannen, D. *You Just Don't Understand: Women and Men in Conversation.* New York: Ballantine Books, 1991.

Tifft, L. L. *Battering of Women: The Failure of Intervention and the Case of Prevention.* Boulder, CO: Westview Press, 1993.

Towers, M. *Self-Esteem: The Power to Be Your Best.* Shawnee Mission, KS: National Press Publications, 1991.

Training Key #246. "Investigating Wife Beating." Police Management and Operations Divisions of the International Association of Chiefs of Police, Inc., Gaithersburg, MD: 1976, 1-5.

Turner, B. F. "Sex Related Differences in Aging." *Handbook of Developmental Psychology.* Edited by B. B. Wolman. Englewood Cliffs, NJ: Prentice-Hall, 1982.

U.S. Department of Justice. *Intimate Victims: A Study of Violence Among Friends and Relatives.* Washington, D.C.: Government Printing Office, 1980.

————. *Uniform Crime Reports for the United States.* Washington, D.C.: U.S. Government Printing Office, 1980.

U.S. Senate Committee on the Judiciary. "Violence against Women: A Week in the Life of America." *Majority Staff Report.* Washington: Government Printing Office, 1992, p. 33.

————. "Hearings on the Treatment of Child Abuse Allegations and Victims in the Judicial and Victims Service System." May 16, 1989. Serial No. J-101-16. S. Hrg. 101-761. Washington, D.C.: U.S. Government Printing Office, 1990.

Walker, L. E. *The Battered Woman Syndrome.* New York: Springer Publishing Co., 1984.

————. *The Battered Woman.* New York: Harper and Row, 1979.

————. "How Battering Happens and How to Stop it." *Battered Women,* Edited by D. Moore. Beverly Hills, CA: Sage Publications, 1979, 59-78.

Walker-Hooper, A. "Domestic Violence: Assessing the Problem." *Conflict Intervention in Social and Domestic Violence.* Edited by C. G. Warner. Bowie, MD: Prentice-Hall, Inc., 1981, 47-85.

Warner, C. G. *Conflict Intervention in Social and Domestic Violence.* New York: Prentice-Hall, Inc., 1981.

Webb, M. "Our Daughters, Ourselves: How Feminists can Raise Feminists." *Ms.,* November/December, 1992, 30-35.

Webster's Ninth New Collegiate Dictionary. Springfield, MA: Merriam-Webster Inc., 1987.

Witt, J. W., Heath, S. M., and Gwinn, C. G. "Domestic Violence Prosecution Protocol." Unpublished Manuscript, San Diego, CA, 1990.

Woititz, J. G. *Healing Your Sexual Self.* Deerfield Beach, FL: Health Communications, Inc., 1989.

Wolfe, J. L. *How to be Sexually Assertive.* New York: GWD Publications, 1976.

Zorza, J. "Woman Battering: A Major Cause of Homelessness." *Clearinghouse Review,* 1991, 25, 421-429.

National Directory of
Domestic Violence Centers

National Coalition Against Domestic Violence (NCADV)
(303) 839-1852

Florida Domestic Violence Hotline
1-800-500-1119
24 hour, Toll-Free, State Wide

Alabama
Alabama Coalition Against Domestic Violence
P. O. Box 4762
Montgomery, AL 36101
(205) 832-4842

Alaska
Alaska Network on Domestic Violence and Sexual Assault
130 Seward St., Room 501
Juneau, AK 99801
(907) 586-3650

Arizona
Arizona Coalition Against Domestic Violence
100 W. Camelback, #109
Phoenix, AZ 85013
(602) 279-2900
1-800-782-6400

Arkansas
Arkansas Coalition Against Violence to Women and Children
7509 Cantrell Rd., Suite 213
Little Rock, AR 72207
(501) 663-4668   1-800-269-4668

Spouse Abuse Shelter
P. O. Box 10594
Clearwater, FL 34617
(813) 344-5555   24-hour helpline (hotline)

Committee to Aid Abused Women
101 15th Street
Sparks, NV 89431
1-800-500-1556 state hotline

California
California Alliance Against Domestic Violence
Marin Abused Women's Services
1717-5th Avenue
San Rafael, CA 94901
(415) 457-2464

Health Resource Center on Domestic Violence
Family Violence Prevention Fund
383 Rhode Island Street, Suite 304
San Francisco, CA 94103-5133
1-800-313-1310   Fax (415) 252-8991

Haven Women's Center of Stanislaus
619 13th Street, Suite 1
Modesto, CA 95354
(209) 577-5980 hotline

Southern California Coalition for Battered Women
P. O. Box 5036
Santa Monica, CA 90409
(213) 655-6098

Canada
National Association of Women and the
Law
604 - 1 Nicholas Street
Ottawa, Ontario, Canada KIN 787
(613) 238-1544

Colorado
Colorado Domestic Violence Coalition
P. O. Box 18902
Denver, CO 80218
(303) 573-9018

Connecticut
Connecticut Coalition Against
Domestic Violence
135 Broad Street
Hartford, CT 06105
(203) 524-5890

Delaware
Delaware Coalition Against Domestic
Violence
507 Philadelphia Pike
Wilmington, DE 19809
(302) 762-6110

Florida
Florida Coalition Against Domestic
Violence
1521A Killearn Center Blvd.
Tallahassee, FL 32308
(904) 668-6862

Florida Coalition Against Domestic
Violence
P. O. Box 5099
Gainesville, FL 32602
(904) 377-8255
1-800-393-SAFE hotline

Georgia
Georgia Advocates for Battered Women
and Children
250 Georgia Avenue, SE, Suite 308
Atlanta, GA 30312
(404) 524-3847   1-800-643-1212

Hawaii
Hawaii State Committee on Family
Violence
2500 Pali Highway
Honolulu, HI 96817
(808) 486-5072

Idaho
Idaho Coalition Against Sexual &
Domestic Violence
200 N. 4th Street, Suite 10-K
Boise, ID 83702
(208) 384-0419

Illinois
Illinois Coalition Against Domestic
Violence
937 South Fourth Street
Springfield, IL 62703
(217) 789-2830

Indiana
Indiana Coalition Against Domestic
Violence
2511 E. 46th Street, Suite N-3
Indianapolis, IN 46205
(317) 543-3908

Iowa
Iowa Coalition Against Domestic Violence
Lucas State Office Bldg. First Floor
Des Moines, IA 50319
(515) 281-7284

Kansas
Kansas Coalition Against Sexual and
Domestic Violence
820 SE Quincy, #416-B
Topeka, KS 66612
(913) 232-9784

Kentucky
Kentucky Domestic Violence Association
P. O. Box 356
Frankfort, KY 40602
(502) 875-4132

Louisiana
Louisiana Coalition Against Domestic
Violence
P. O. Box 3053
Hammond, LA 70404
(504) 542-4446

Maine
Maine Coalition for Family Crisis Services
P. O. Box 89
Winterport, ME 04496
(207) 941-1194

Maryland
Maryland Network Against Domestic
Violence
11501 Georgia Avenue, #403
Silver Spring, MD 20902
(301) 942-0900

Massachusetts
Massachusetts Coalition of Battered
Women's Service Groups
210 Commercial Street, 3rd Floor
Boston, MA 02109
(617) 248-0922

National Committee for the Prevention
of Elder Abuse
c/o Institute on Aging
Medical Center of Central Massachusetts
119 Belmont Street
Worcester, MA 01605
(508) 793-6166

Michigan
Michigan Coalition Against Domestic
Violence
P. O. Box 16009
Lansing, MI 48901
(517) 484-2924

Minnesota
Minnesota Coalition for Battered Women
1619 Dayton Avenue, #303
St. Paul, MN 55104
(612) 646-6177

Battered Women's Justice Project
Minnesota Program Development, Inc.
206 West Fourth Street
Duluth, MN 55806
1-800-903-0111
Fax (218) 722-1545

Mississippi
Gulf Coast Battered Women's Center
P. O. Box 333
Biloxi, MS 39533
(601) 436-3809

Mississippi Coalition Against
Domestic Violence
P.O. Box 4703
Jackson, MS 39296-4703
(601) 981-9196

Missouri
Missouri Coalition Against Domestic
Violence
331 Madison Street
Jefferson City, MO 65101
(314) 634-4161

National Organization for Changing Men
RAVEN
7314 Manchester, 2nd Floor
St Louis, MO 63143
(314) 645-2075

Nevada
Nevada Network Against Domestic
Violence
2100 Capurro Way, Suite E
Sparks, NV 89431
(702) 358-1171
1-800-500-1556 state hotline

New Hampshire
New Hampshire Coalition Against
Domestic and Sexual Violence
P. O. Box 353
Concord, NH 03302-0353
(603) 224-8893
1-800-852-3388 state hotline

New Jersey
New Jersey Coalition for Battered
Women
2620 Whitehorse Hamilton Square Rd.
Trenton, NJ 08690
(609) 584-8107
1-800-572-7233 state hotline

New Mexico
New Mexico State Coalition Against
Domestic Violence
P. O. Box 25363
Albuquerque, NM 87125
(505) 246-924
1-800 773-3645 state hotline

New York
New York State Coalition Against
Domestic Violence
Women's Bldg., 79 Central Ave.
Albany, NY 12206
(518) 432-4864
1-800-942-6906 Eng.
1-800-942-6908 Span.

North Carolina
North Carolina Coalition Against
Domestic Violence
P. O. Box 51875
Durham, NC 27717
(919) 956-9124

North Dakota
North Dakota Council on Abused
Women's Services
418 E. Rosser Avenue, #320
Bismarck, ND 58501
(701) 255-6240
1-800-472-2911 state hotline

Ohio
Action Ohio Coalition for Battered
Women
P. O. Box 15673
Columbus, OH 43215
(614) 221-1255
1-800-934-9840

Ohio Domestic Violence Network
4041 N High Street, # 101
Columbus, OH 43214
(614) 784-0023
1-800-934-9840

Oklahoma
Oklahoma Coalition on Domestic Violence
and Sexual Assault
2200 Classen Blvd., #1300
Oklahoma City, OK 73106
(405) 557-1210

Oregon

Oregon Coalition Against Domestic and
Sexual Violence
520 NW Davis, Suite 310
Portland, OR 97209
(503) 223-7411
1-800-OCA-DSV2

Pennsylvania

Pennsylvania Coalition Against Domestic
Violence
& National Resource Center
6400 Flank Drive, #1300
Harrisburg, PA 17112
(717) 545-6400
1-800-932-4632 state hotline

National Resource Center on Domestic
Violence
Pennsylvania Coalition Against Violence
6400 Flank Drive, Suite 1300
Harrisburg, PA 17112
1-800-537-2238
Fax 717-545-9456

National Clearinghouse for the Defense
of Battered Women
125 South 9th Street, Suite 302
Philadelphia, PA 19107
(215) 351-0010
Fax (215) 357-0779

Puerto Rico

Comision Para Los Asuntos
De La Mujer
Calle San Fracisco 151-153
Viejo San Juan
San Juan, Puerto Rico 00905
(809) 722-2907

Rhode Island

Rhode Island Council on Domestic
Violence
324 Broad Street
Central Falls, RI 02863
(401) 723-3051

St. Croix

Women's Coalition of St. Croix
Box 2734
Christiansted
St. Croix, VI 00822
(809) 773-9272 hotline

St. Thomas/St. John

Women's Resource Center Inc.
8 Kongens Gade
St. Thomas, VI 00802
(809) 776-7867 hotline

South Carolina

South Carolina Coalition Against
Domestic Violence and Sexual Assault
P. O. Box 7776
Columbia, SC 29202
(803) 254-3699

South Dakota

South Dakota Coalition Against Domestic
Violence and Sexual Assault
3220 S. Hwy. 281
Aberdeen, SD 57401
(605) 225-5122

Tennessee

Tennessee Task Force Against Family
Violence
P. O. Box 120972
Nashville, TN 37212-0972
(615) 386-9406
1-800-356-6767 (state hotline)

Texas

Texas Council on Family Violence
8701 N. Mopac Expressway, #450
Austin, TX 78759
(512) 794-1133
1-800-525-1978 National hotline

Vermont
Vermont Network Against Domestic
Violence and Sexual Assault
P. O. Box 405
Montpelier, VT 05601
(802) 223-1302

Virginia
Virginians Against Domestic Violence
2850 Sandy Bay Rd., #101
Williamsburg, VA 23185
(804) 221-0990
1-800-838-8238

Washington
Washington State Coalition Against
Domestic Violence
200 "W". Street SE, Suite B
Tumwater, WA 98501
(206) 352-4029
1-800-562-6025 state hotline

Washington, D.C.
DC Coalition Against Domestic Violence
P. O. Box 76069
Washington, DC 20013
(202) 783-5332

National Council on Child Abuse and
Family Violence
1155 Connecticut Avenue, NW
Suite 400
Washington, DC 20036
(202) 429-6695 or 1-800-222-2000

West Virginia
West Virginia Coalition Against
Domestic Violence
P. O. Box 85
181 B. Main Street
Sutton, WV 26601
(304) 765-2250

Wisconsin
Wisconsin Coalition Against Domestic
Violence
1400 E. Washington Avenue, #103
Madison, WI 53703
(608) 255-0539

Wyoming
Wyoming Self-help Center
341 East E. Street, #135A
Casper, WY 82601
(307) 235-2814
1-800-990-3877

Wyoming Coalition Against Domestic
Violence and Sexual Assault
341 East E. Street, #135A
Casper, WY 82601
(307) 266-4334
1-800-990-3877

Index

Profile of the Author

Dr. V. Michael McKenzie is a practicing psychologist, and Adjunct Professor of Psychology at Saint Leo College in Florida. He holds an A.A., and a B.A., from the City University of New York; a M.Ed., and C.A.S., from Harvard University; a M.S.Sc., and Ph.D., from Syracuse University. He was a Teaching Fellow in Psychology at Harvard, and a Psychology Instructor at Syracuse University. He has published numerous scholarly articles in professional journals, and was Consulting Editor for the Ophthalmology Management Magazine. Dr. McKenzie was Clinical Director of the Medical Services Department's EAP at the New York City Transit Authority from 1986 through 1992. The author served in the U.S. Army during the Vietnam War.

In August of 1994, Governor Lawton Chiles appointed Dr. McKenzie to the Commission on Minimum Standards for Batterers' Treatment. This Commission was established by the Florida State Legislature, and charged with developing treatment standards for spousal batterers in the State of Florida.

To order additional copies of this book, please use coupon below.

Mail to:

Brunswick Publishing Corporation
1386 LAWRENCEVILLE PLANK ROAD
LAWRENCEVILLE, VIRGINIA 23868

Order Form

Please send me _____ copy(s) of *Domestic Violence in America* by
V. Michael McKenzie, ISBN 1-55618-151-5, at $29.95 per copy plus $5.00
mailing and handling for the first copy, 50 cents for each additional copy.
Virginia residents add $1.35 sales tax.

❑ Check enclosed.   Charge Orders only: — 1-800-336-7154

❑ Charge to my credit card:
   ❑ VISA   ❑ MasterCard   ❑ American Express

Tel: 804-848-3865 • Fax: 804-848-0607

Card #_____ Exp. Date_____

Signature: _____

Name _____

Address _____

City_____ State_____ Zip _____

Phone # _____